Faithful Dissenters

Stories of Men and Women
Who Loved and Changed the Church

Robert McClory

ORBIS BOOKS

Maryknoll, New York 10545

Fourth printing, December 2001

The Catholic Foreign Mission Society of America (Maryknoll) recruits and trains people for overseas missionary service. Through Orbis Books, Maryknoll aims to foster the international dialogue that is essential to mission. The books published, however, reflect the opinions of their authors and are not meant to represent the official position of the society. To obtain more information about Maryknoll and Orbis Books, please visit our website at www.maryknoll.org.

Published in 2000 by
Orbis Books
P.O. Box 308
Maryknoll, New York 10545-0308

Photograph credits — John Courtney Murray: Georgetown University Library Special Collections Division; Portrait of Galileo by Ottavio Leoni: Scala/Art Resource, New York; John Henry Newman: Maryknoll Photo Library; Mary Ward: Institute of the Blessed Virgin Mary; "The Money-Changer and His Wife" by Marinus van Reymerswaele: Erich Lessing/Art Resource; Ex-voto of Saint Catherine of Siena: Giraudon/Art Resource, New York; Matteo Ricci: Galerie Illustrée de la Compagnie de Jesus, Paris/Loyola University Chicago Archives; Hildegard of Bingen: Robert Lentz, 1997; Yves Congar: Catholic News Service; Portrait of Saint Thomas Aquinas by Fra Bartolomeo: Nicolo Orsi Battaglini/Art Resource, New York; Mother Theodore Guerin: Sisters of Providence of St.-Mary-of-the-Woods, Indiana. Cover photo of painting "Galileo Galilei before the Inquisition" by François Richard Fleury courtesy of Erich Lessing/Art Resource, New York.

Manufactured in the United States of America.

Library of Congress Cataloging-in-Publication Data

McClory, Robert, 1932-
    Faithful dissenters : stories of men and women who loved and changed the church / Robert McClory
        p. cm.
    Includes bibliographical references and index.
    ISBN 1-57075-322-9 (pbk.)
    1. Catholics – History. 2. Dissenters, Religious – History. 3. Catholic Church – Doctrines – History. I. Title.
BX4669 .M24 2000
282'.092'2 – dc21
[B]

                                                         00-032689

CONTENTS

ACKNOWLEDGMENTS

This book was inspired in large measure by a small volume of 103 pages — an essay really — written by John Henry Newman and entitled *On Consulting the Faithful in Matters of Doctrine.* Newman wrote it when he was subjected to criticism and discipline for insisting that the creation of Church doctrine is not the exclusive preserve of the hierarchy and that consultation with the laity is, in fact, a necessity for authentic doctrine. His goal was to demonstrate that at least during one period of Church history it was the laity, not the hierarchy, who maintained orthodox doctrine. And he did so with the flourish of scholarship for which he was well known. Were there, I wondered as I read his account, other occasions when official Church doctrine or discipline had been "corrected" by Catholics outside the hierarchy? Far from being an exceptional situation, I discovered, such correction forms a constant and integral part of Church history, though it goes largely unmentioned in the official annals. I am therefore especially grateful to Newman for opening up to me this fascinating vista.

I am also grateful to the other authors noted throughout this book who did not attempt to politely pass over the constructive contributions of responsible dissenters. And I'm likewise thankful to the many people who recommended dissenters and who recommended (or loaned) books or suggested fertile areas for investigation. Among them are James Orgren, Gary Macy, Charles Curran, William LaDue, Michael McGillicuddy, Judy Schoenherr, Judy Cates, Anna Bockstegen, Don Wedd, Ann Bond, R.S.J., Michael Leach, Robert Ludwig, the Sisters of the Institute of the Blessed Virgin Mary and the Sisters of Providence of St. Mary of the Woods, George Hinger, Meinrad Scherer-Emunds, Brother Michael Grace, S.J., Bernard Cooke, and Dean Ryerson. Thanks also goes to Ken Bode, dean of the Medill School of Journalism at Northwestern University, and the Wade Nichols Research Fund for assistance in writing and research and to David Nimrod and the staff at the United Library of Garrett-Evangelical and Seabury-Western Theological Schools. Extremely helpful in the preliminary editing process were my daughter, Jennifer, and my brother, Eugene. Serving well above and beyond the call of duty throughout the creation of this book was my wife, Margaret.

A RICH TRADITION

There is a moment in the play *The Miracle Worker* that had a profound effect on me. It was not the great climax — powerful though it is — when the blind and deaf girl, Helen Keller, for the first time in her life understands that signs stand for things. She realizes in a flash that the signs her teacher Annie Sullivan has been tracing on her hand for months are an alphabet by which, through touch, she can at last communicate with the world outside; her trapped mind is liberated.

The moment that struck me occurs earlier in the drama and happens so quickly during an argument between Sullivan and Helen's father that it can pass almost unnoticed. For months, Sullivan has been attempting to break through, to open the girl's mind, but without success. Helen remains willful and wild, and the Keller family is prepared to give up hope, to place her in an institution for the mentally retarded. Sullivan pleads for more time in which to impart to Helen "new eyes" through this touch alphabet. Speaking from his own experience, the wisdom of age, and his acceptance of limitation, Helen's father says, "Perhaps God may not have meant Helen to have the eyes you speak of." And Sullivan retorts, "*I* mean her to!"[1]

I was shocked. What arrogance, I thought, what stubbornness! How could this woman so easily contradict the obvious? What did she know? But I was instantly faced with another question: Where was God in this moment? In the wisdom and experience of the father, or in the arrogant determination of Sullivan?

If we may presume that God wills his creatures to reach their full potential if at all possible, then I had to admit that, of course, God was with the dissenter, Annie Sullivan, in her stubborn determination. Subsequent events in the real life of Helen Keller speak volumes: the development of her mind, her years of achievement and inspiration all over the world, and her contributions to the cause of the disabled. Annie Sullivan was vindicated.

This is not a book about Annie Sullivan. But it is about dissenters, people who were like her in some ways. It concerns some of those who, down through the centuries of Catholicism, have dared to contradict and criticize the voice of authority. Many, in one way or another, were charged with arrogance, disrespect of authority, or worse. But in the light of subsequent events, they have been vindicated — in the eyes of history and in the eyes of the Church.

•

"Dissent" is not usually considered a complimentary word. It resembles other "dis" words like "disagreement," "disobedience," and "disgrace." To dissent from legitimate authority is to stand apart, to place oneself in opposition to established norms, regulations, decrees. Authority, by its very definition, does not favor dissent. It views dissent as a threat to good order, and worries that, if carried too far, it may destroy the foundations on which an institution is built. Since Catholics see the Church as founded by God's will on the authority of Jesus Christ, dissent of any kind carries certain ominous, troubling overtones. In the modern era, Church authority has taken an especially dim view of dissent, reiterating the necessity of internal and external assent to Church teachings, even taking strong disciplinary action against a variety of dissenting individuals.

Yet, dissent is still widespread, even pandemic, in today's Church. It concerns such well-known matters as the ban on artificial contraception, the prohibition against women priests, the celibacy requirement for the priesthood, the condemnation of homosexual activity, and the rejection of marriage after divorce. These and more are extremely hot buttons in modern Catholicism. And all of them raise certain questions of principle over which Catholics remain in disagreement:

- Is it possible that a long-accepted tradition or an interpretation of Sacred Scripture may be erroneously expressing God's design, or does the Church's stamp of approval guarantee the truth?

- Does the obligation of obedience to legitimate Church authority always take precedence over innovative response in certain situations, or is there room for exception?

- Is the nonacceptance of a Church doctrine by great numbers of Catholics over a long period of time a sure sign of rampant infidelity, or is it a call for reconsideration by Church authority?

- Is dissent by its very nature disruptive of good order, or are there situations when it creates a greater good?

There are countless books and articles on both sides of these questions, and they have provoked interminable discussions and arguments. I have been involved in many such debates myself. And I've found that discussions of principle invariably lead to frustrating stalemates. Arguments over the concrete issues of dissent today seem only to reinforce previous convictions. So this book does not deal directly with any of that. Nor does it consider the particular situations of well-known dissenters who represent these various positions. It is an attempt to clear the air by stepping back several paces and considering concrete instances of dissent from the past, concentrating on the persons who dissented, what they did, why they did it, and what their legacy is.

The persons I have selected here have several things in common: they are dead; they remained in the Church through thick and thin; they did not reject the concept of Church authority; the issues over which they dissented are now resolved; and the Church (in some cases, the world) is better for their contribution. But there is wide variety in time, place, and circumstance. Some dissenters spoke out in the clearest terms, asserting that doctrines long taught at the highest levels of authority and universally accepted as fully grounded in Scripture and tradition were wrong; among these were matters generally regarded at the time as irreformable and in no way open to revision. Other dissenters disputed the stated positions of bishops or popes. Some treated certain Church mandates as if they did not exist. And some pushed at the limits of Church authority by other means until they gave way.

The relative scarcity of women among these dissenters must be noted. This is not because women remained ever compliant — quite the contrary. But since women were (and are) essentially excluded from decision-making roles and major public offices in the Church, their dissent has usually fallen, as it were, beneath the radar of Church authorities.

This book is not meant to encourage dissent as a general practice. Throughout history, Church authority in countless instances has followed a course that was wise and prudent, leading to outcomes that can only be considered providential. As a general rule, I believe, Catholics should give that authority the benefit of the doubt. But the Church is a human as well as divine institution; it is not always and everywhere protected from mistaken judgment, premature decision, or the other errors and foibles to which the exercise of authority on this earth is subject.

It cannot be predicted that all the current dissent controversies will prove beneficial to the Church in the long run, as have those reported here. There is no doubt that dissent in the history of the Church has sometimes led to heresies, wars, and persecutions, and unfortunately, those are the instances we more often hear about. But as the cases reviewed in these chapters show, dissent can also be an important vehicle for something else — for providing new insights, for correcting past errors, for enriching the Church. History says that there's good dissent and there's bad dissent, just as in other contexts there's good cholesterol and there's bad cholesterol, good liturgy and bad liturgy, good administration and bad administration.

Some have suggested that the Church of the twenty-first century needs a theology of dissent. Such a theology would begin with the recognition that quiet, passive submission is not always the appropriate response in ecclesial disputes. It would also recognize that dissent can become a vehicle for self-indulgence or an outlet for lingering resentments. Still, such a theology would urge the important contribution of respectful dissent, and it would promote the settlement of differences through dialogue, prayer, and further study rather than through the muzzling of discussion. Before he became Pope John Paul II, Karol Wojtyla wrote in *The Acting Person* that moral growth in any community requires a creative tension between two poles: solidarity and opposition. "The structure of a human community is correct," he said, "only if it admits not just the presence of a justified opposition but also that practical effectiveness of opposition required by the common good."

The accounts here can be read simply as narratives of interesting people caught up in complex, conflicted situations. Far more appropriately, I think, they can be studied for the light they shed on the hot buttons mentioned above. In the long run, it is the task of theologians and analytical historians to make insightful connections, to point out precisely where past and present intersect. Yet, no one needs special training to realize that history repeats itself. Indeed, history ought to be a special teacher for Catholics, whose faith is based not just on Scripture but on the presence of the Holy Spirit in tradition as well. And tradition means history—from the time of Christ up to and including the era of the internet. Ours is a rich tradition, full of odd turns and surprises as unexpected as the blind seeing and the deaf hearing.

ONE

JOHN COURTNEY MURRAY

Religious Freedom Triumphant

He died in a New York taxicab on his way from his sister's home to his office at the LaFarge Institute. The date was August 16, 1967. He was sixty-two years old. His sudden death stunned the public, but it was not a surprise to those who knew him well. John Courtney Murray had endured a series of heart attacks over the previous twelve years, each one a little more severe. Eighteen months before, while recovering from one of those episodes, he had what he called the happiest day of his life when invited to concelebrate Mass with Pope Paul VI. It was a joyous liturgy, followed by dinner, champagne, and toasts—for him, for his achievement.

Some have said that he gave his life for the cause; all his energy had gone into it, and now there was nothing left. Murray would not have called it a cause, but that's what it had become, and he simply had to see it through to the finish.

The issue was the teaching of the Catholic Church on the proper relationship of church and state, particularly regarding freedom of worship. Deeply entrenched in Catholic tradition was the conviction that the state had an obligation to recognize the Catholic Church in its constitution, to give it preferential treatment in public affairs, and to suppress whatever or whoever opposed the Church or its teachings.

That position was called the "Catholic Thesis," and it was considered not subject to alteration.

This arrangement supposed that the vast majority (if not all) of the citizens of the state were Catholic — which was actually the case in Europe almost from the fourth century until the time of the Protestant Reformation. It appeared logical that since the Catholic religion was the true, divinely revealed religion for all people, those who publicly professed contrary views were in a state of error — and error has no rights. Just as someone who yells "Fire!" in a crowded theater without cause puts the patrons in danger, so the heretic or schismatic was seen as recklessly endangering the faith of the people; for the common good, such a person must be silenced.

But since the upheavals of the Reformation and the French Revolution, many European governments were no longer majority Catholic and no longer governed by Catholic monarchs. How the Church and how Catholic citizens ought to react to these situations became a matter of worry and discussion. The answer, decided Church authorities in the eighteenth and nineteenth centuries, was to tolerate non-Catholic states until such time as the Catholic population grew into the majority. The Church, in other words, would forgo its right to legal establishment as the true religion but would give no approval of the existing situation. That pragmatic position came to be known as the "Catholic Hypothesis."

Meanwhile, there was a trend among European governments not only to distance themselves from the Church but also to become aggressively antireligion. The term "freedom of religion" came to mean "freedom from religion," and "separation of church and state" in some places meant "antagonism of state toward church." The trend, commonly referred to as "Continental Liberalism," alarmed a series of popes who warned the faithful of the dangers of secularism and extolled the virtues of the Catholic Thesis as the only acceptable form of church-state relationship.

The situation in the United States was different. Here was a democratic government that did not recognize Catholicism, yet was in principle neither anti-Catholic nor antireligion. In fact, Catholicism was flourishing in America. Still, in Rome there was a fear that in this unregulated new republic Catholics and non-Catholics were getting along too well, and that eventually American Catholicism would be watered down, secularized, and transformed into some variation of Continental Liberalism.

Pope Pius IX had been quite clear, declaring in his 1847 *Syllabus of Errors* that states must recognize the Catholic religion as supreme, must put their power at the Church's disposal, and must punish or compel those who do not conform to Church requirements. In the last years of the nineteenth century, Pope Leo XIII specifically upheld the Catholic Thesis as the ideal for America. In his 1895 encyclical, *Longinqua oceani,* addressed to U.S. bishops, Leo said, "It would be very dangerous to draw the conclusion that in America is to be sought...the most desirable status of the Church....She [the U.S. Church] would bring forth more abundant fruits if, in addition to liberty, she enjoyed the favor of the laws and the patronage of the public authority." The further dangers of a watered-down Catholicism Leo assessed in his 1899 encyclical, *Testem benevolentiae.* He spoke of errors, "called by some Americanism," that may lead Catholics to treat certain doctrines "as if of lesser moment" or to give new meanings to teachings that "the Church has invariably held."[1]

For the next fifty years, no theologian of note disputed the Catholic Thesis as an ideal. The tradition was clear, the popes explicit; there was no room for movement. But among American Catholics there was a great uneasiness — and not a little embarrassment. Their non-Catholic associates could insist, "You tolerate us until you become the majority in this country or possibly until you get a Catholic president. Then our religious views will be repressed just as they are in a Catholic country like Spain." This was precisely the Protestant argument when a Catholic, Al Smith, ran for the presidency in 1928; he was soundly defeated. Catholics had no convincing rebuttal; their Church's position was fixed and irreversible — until John Courtney Murray.

Rarely in Church history has a doctrine undergone such a profound development — many would say reversal — in such a short time. In a period of about fifteen years (1950–65), the Catholic Thesis was disestablished and freedom of religion was set in place as the governing principle in the Church's relations with the modern world. Murray was surely the principal agent in effecting change, but the power behind it, the evidence behind Murray's argument, was the sense of the faithful — the American Catholic faithful — whose experience in a situation of total religious freedom opened up a whole new way to view an old reality.

THE PRELIMINARY BOUT

John Courtney Murray was a tall, handsome man with a commanding presence and a mind that could, like a buzz saw, cut through a mass of detail to identify the salient point. He was born in New York City in 1904 of immigrant parents, his mother from Ireland, his father from Scotland. As a youth, he thought of studying medicine, but the family lacked funds for advanced education. He joined the Jesuit religious order at sixteen, and following the usual, extended course of study and formation, he was ordained a priest in 1933. He taught for a time at the Jesuit Woodstock College seminary in Maryland, then was named both editor of *Theological Studies* magazine and religion editor of *America* magazine in the early 1940s. In 1946 he was a founding board member of the Catholic Theological Society of America. He thus became quickly acquainted with the society's first president, Redemptorist Fr. Francis Connell, and the first secretary, Msgr. Joseph Fenton, both professors at the Catholic University of America and both associated with the *American Ecclesiastical Review* magazine. In the years to come Fenton and, to a lesser extent, Connell would become his most bitter opponents in the battle over freedom of religion. As his contribution to the new board, Murray was asked to probe the idea of an authoritative Church in a democracy. He agreed, his interests were honed, and his course for the next twenty years was set.

Murray approached intellectual issues head-on with the zeal of a missionary, determined to master every inch of his subject. As he told his Jesuit superior, "If we are to interpret the world, as we must, even to itself, our first duty is to understand it, in detail, with full realism under abnegation of the easy generalities with which the world is ordinarily denounced."[2]

In 1947 he made national headlines for the first time when he engaged in a debate with Dean Walter Russell Bowie of New York's Union Theological Seminary; the text was later published in *American Mercury* magazine. Bowie pushed the hot buttons and kept his finger on them throughout the match. Quoting several papal documents, he said that Protestants have every reason to "believe that the clearly stated Roman Catholic purpose to make America Catholic would jeopardize the religious and civil liberties which have been the glory of Protestant countries and of Protestant culture." His greatest fear, said Bowie, is the Church's claim to "dominance wherever it can assert and maintain its claims." Murray likened Bowie's evidence "to the bone or two out of which the Sunday-supplement archeologist constructs the museum-piece prehistoric monster." He acknowledged that Bowie had a few scattered bones, but added, "I have more sense than to regard past Catholic documents on church and state as so many crystal balls in which to discern the shape of things to come."[3] The debate produced scores of letters on both sides of the issue and served as a kind of public springboard for the debate to come within the Church.

In trying to reformulate the Church's position on church-state and human freedom, Murray was taking on an apparently impregnable fortress protected by several centuries of tradition and a moat of papal decrees. Just as he began his task, yet another document in the papal series appeared. Pope Pius XII, in his 1950 encyclical, *Humani generis,* rebuked (without naming names) anyone who promotes new doctrines and novel ideas. Fenton, who accepted the Catholic Thesis on church-state relations as a virtually infallible dogma, argued that this at last should end any speculation about re-formation. "The truth that the state, like every other human society, is objectively obligated to worship God according to the one religion God has established and commanded is so obviously a part of Catholic doctrine," wrote Fenton, "that no theologian has any excuse to call it into question.... When the Holy Father gives his decision on any subject which has hitherto been subject to controversy, his judgment is no longer open to question."[4]

In 1951 Murray's first article specifically dealing with church, state, and freedom was published in the *American Ecclesiastical Review.* He went back to Leo XIII, quoted the pope extensively, and suggested that Leo, like many who designed the Catholic Thesis-Hypothesis concept, had addressed church and state solely in the abstract without noticing how the issue was working itself out in the concrete. The problem was being solved in the United States, he said, "but the din raised by the conflict with Continental Liberalism was too great to permit the voice of America...to be heard in European canon-law classrooms."

Fenton accused Murray of being ambiguous and using vague terminology. Connell joined in, charging Murray with trying to smooth the way toward a better understanding of the Catholic Church on the part of non-Catholics in America "by compromising Catholic principles or concealing them" — the very evil Leo XIII had categorized as Americanism. Murray replied, with a touch of sarcasm, that Connell was "nostalgic for the dear dead days of the Catholic state on the monarchic or dictatorial model!" Connell's single concern, said Murray, is "for the powers of the powers, not for the freedoms of the people. And he considers the theory and practice of Church-State relations to be 'all finished.' There is no more problem; it has been solved. Leo XIII said the last word. The theologian's task is that of repetition of what has been said. He has not to search, explore, explain, develop; he has simply to impose the finished formula."

This, as it turned out, was just the preliminary bout.

OPPOSITION FROM ROME

From 1951 through 1954 Murray developed his theory principally through four long articles in *Theological Studies*. The product was a dense, exhaustive treatise in which he sought to demonstrate that the Church's doctrine on freedom had been so influenced by historical circumstances that it overlooked an entire aspect of the issue, namely, the fundamental inviolability of human freedom and the supremacy of conscience, even an ill-informed conscience. Scrutinizing the writings of Leo XIII and Pius XII, he saw a dawning, as yet inchoate, recognition of that aspect, even though the contrary appeared more often in their much-quoted encyclicals. Murray's final position can be summed up (in extremely simplified form) under three points:[5]

• "Every human person is endowed with a dignity that surpasses the rest of creatures because the human person is independent... responsible for self and autonomous. The primordial demand of dignity then is that man acts by his own counsel and purpose, using and enjoying his freedom, moved not by external coercion, but internally by the risk of his whole existence." People are responsible for who they become and whether they achieve their destiny or not. "So great is this dignity that not even God can take it away — by taking upon himself or unto himself the responsibility for man's life and his fate."

• The primary purpose of all social institutions, including government, is to service and support human dignity and freedom. Their purpose is not to promote religious truth or to give it special privilege, since "the truth to which government is accountable is the truth of human dignity." These institutions must respect that people are responsible for themselves. Therefore it is impossible to speak of having respect for the inner moral and religious freedom of persons while at the same time prohibiting the public exercise of that freedom. "The juridical order cannot be sundered from the moral order any more than the human person can be halved."

• Freedom is to be restricted only in those rare instances where the public peace or justice is threatened. All persons are to be regarded by social institutions as "equal in dignity and nature, and all are equally the subject and foundation of human society."

In effect, Murray said, the old Catholic Thesis, which made government the servant of the Church, was anachronistic. It had been outmoded by fresh insight coming out of the historical experience of modern democracy, particularly the kind of democracy found in the United States. Here, he said, the Church had "a new kind of spiritual existence, not tested on the Continent — the experience of reliance on its own inner resources under a regime of constitutional law that has been equitable . . . but not creative of legal privilege."

Murray insisted that he did not present these views as a new Catholic Thesis, an ideal for all times and places. Doctrine develops, he insisted, because a person's hold on objective truth is always partial, always limited; and progress can occur only if people are allowed to live "in a zone of freedom."[6]

Throughout the four years of development, Msgr. Fenton continually sniffed the sulfuric odor of heresy in all this, and he shared his fears far and wide, in the pages of the *American Ecclesiastical Review*, in speeches and letters, and in appeals to Rome. In March of 1953 he got major support. Cardinal Alfredo Ottaviani, head of the Holy Office, delivered a speech in which he upheld the Catholic Thesis as official Church doctrine; he insisted that only those governments that recognize and defer to the Church are consistent with a long tradition and with Pope Leo's interpretation of that tradition. He did not mention Murray and didn't have to; Murray was the only theologian in the world at the time reevaluating Leo's views.

This represented a rebuke from the man closest to the pope, and the import of the message was not lost on Murray or on his Jesuit superiors. One month after Ottaviani's talk, Murray was hospitalized in Baltimore for extreme fatigue due to cardiac insufficiency and was forced to take a two-month rest. Nevertheless, in June one of the most important articles on his theory appeared in *Theological Studies.* Fenton was quick to retaliate. "The very concept of sacred theology itself is completely misrepresented," he said, "when nationality, American or any other, is depicted as an effective factor in determining theological opinions."[7]

Murray had few allies in his effort to recast doctrine, one of them being Msgr. John Tracy Ellis of the Catholic University of America, the best-known and most prolific Catholic historian in the United States. Writing to Ellis in mid-1953, Murray expressed his discouragement that the American hierarchy and influential writers like Fenton remained frozen in a defensive, post-Reformation state of mind. "I do not indeed want the American situation canonized as 'ideal'," he said. "It would be enough if it could be defended as legitimate in principle, as standing [equally]... with the Spanish situation — each representing an important realization of principle in divergent historical contexts."

Ellis urged him to "go cautiously but with calm courage."[8]

EVER DARKENING SKIES

In the wake of the Ottaviani speech, anti-Murray articles began to appear in European theological journals. In November of 1953 Fr. Vincent McCormick, a representative of the Jesuit general superior in Rome, forwarded to Murray an enigmatic *mandatum* (order), indicating that the trouble had spread to the highest level of the religious order. "I think the time has come for Fr. Murray to put down in simple, clear statements his full, present position regarding this Church-State question," said McCormick, "and to send it to me for Father General."[9]

Murray replied that he would respond in detail, but "it so happens that I haven't yet the energy to undertake more than one major task at a time." He added that he did not so much have a position at that time but "a purpose of inquiry," and wondered if he was actually suspected of heresy or "simply the object of interest." McCormick then softened his tone and promised to advise Murray at once and clearly if any direct threat were forthcoming.

Murray recovered some of his self-confidence when he had dinner with two influential American prelates, Cardinals Edward Mooney of Detroit and Samuel Stritch of Chicago. Both listened "sympathetically," he reported to McCormick, and Stritch said that he was glad someone was coping with the knotty issues relating to religious freedom.

In December, Pope Pius XII entered the arena in an allocution, *Ci riesce,* to a group of Italian judges; its content, however, was so ambiguous it could be interpreted several ways. Fenton reacted quickly. *Ci riesce* should end further discussion, he said, since it clearly establishes "the legitimacy of the explanation of relations between church and state in terms of thesis and hypothesis." Furthermore, declared Fenton, the allocution shows that the expression "error has no rights" is still applicable regarding non-Catholic religions.

The new year, 1954, saw the controversy enter a period of open warfare. In March, Murray gave his own, very different interpretation of the papal allocution in a speech at the Catholic University of America (CUA). Oddly enough, no copies or transcriptions of that talk were preserved, so researchers were reduced to speculations based on Murray's notes and summaries by others. He said, his notes indicated, that *Ci riesce* was, in fact, a rebuke of Ottaviani's speech, since Pius affirmed that he, the pope, and only he, is competent to speak out on vital questions affecting church and state. The pope really intended, in Murray's view, to counter Ottaviani in every way; therefore, his notes stated, "Anyone whose theory is that of Ottaviani is under necessity of reversing his views."

The CUA speech was a decisive moment in the debate, for Murray had underestimated either the pope's real intent or Ottaviani's power, or both. Said Murray biographer Donald Pelotte, "Murray's outright and public criticism of Ottaviani would prove to be the real turning point in the controversy. The argument with Rome on the Church and State issue might have followed in any event. But this made it inevitable and, for Ottaviani, made it personal."[10]

Fenton called the CUA speech "utterly baseless." Those who would like to believe "that authoritative pontifical teaching on this and other subjects has changed or 'developed' in such a way that some things presented as true by [the popes] have been completely or partially denied by more recent pontiffs would not like what Ottaviani had to say on the subject. *Ci riesce,* however, gives no support to this opposition."

One week after the CUA talk, Ottaviani personally contacted New York Cardinal Francis Spellman, urging him to discuss Murray's beliefs with his Jesuit superiors. In the following months, pressure was brought to bear on several fronts. The head of the Holy Cross religious order was asked to persuade Fr. Theodore Hesburgh, president of the University of Notre Dame, to cancel a lecture by Murray scheduled at the school. Hesburgh did not cooperate. But a book containing an essay by Murray and ready for publication by Notre Dame Press was canceled due to complaints from Roman officials. A speech on church-state relations to be delivered in Rome by Murray's friend, John Tracy Ellis, was also canceled because of Vatican opposition.

Murray was deeply distressed by the assault, telling McCormick that he was pessimistic about what he had stirred up and had little inclination to complete the final *Theological Studies* article in the series on his theory. Then came a new blow from Rome. In *Si diligis,* yet another allocution (before an international group of cardinals and bishops), Pope Pius scolded "those who care little for conformity with the living Teaching Authority of the Church, pay little heed for her commonly received doctrine...and at the same time they follow their own bent too much, and regard too highly the...standards of other branches of learning."[11] Fenton was ecstatic, counting *Si diligis* "among the more important doctrinal declarations of modern times." The teaching in statements like this one and *Ci riesce,* he wrote, are authoritative expressions of the pope's ordinary magisterium and must be assented to by all Catholics, under pain of mortal sin.

Murray struggled on nevertheless, completing in early 1955 his final *Theological Studies* piece, which he regarded as the crucial capstone of his entire theory. He sent the article to Rome for review by the Jesuit censors and asked permission to go to Rome himself, presumably to make his case in person. McCormick advised against a trip, since it might arouse publicity. The Holy Office, he said, is "just now . . . rather on edge," and Cardinal Ottaviani "has been too badly hurt by this whole affair."

SILENCED

In July the inevitable occurred. McCormick informed Murray that the censors had rejected his article, and the Jesuit general, on orders from the Holy Office, was silencing Murray indefinitely on topics of church and state. His views were under censure and could not be printed or reprinted under any circumstances. Nothing would be gained, Mc-Cormick said, by resisting and further "provoking those who will not be appeased."[12]

Murray thanked McCormick for his delicate way of saying, "You're through!" but added, "The whole thing represents a defeat and failure of the first order." He later wrote, "All the books on Church and State and on allied topics have been cleared from my room, in symbol of my retirement, which I expect to be permanent." He asked what topics he could write about, and McCormick said, "I suppose you may write poetry. Between harmless poetry and Church-State problems, what fields are taboo I don't know."

Never one to share his emotions with great openness, Murray did not comment on the impatience he felt during the next three years. He began writing about the challenges of pluralism facing the Church in America, while steering clear of any church-state comments. But late in 1957 he could control his frustration no longer as he looked at that final, unpublished article summing up more than six years of work. Murray sent copies to the rector at Woodstock College, suggesting that the substance of the piece could and should be published as long as there were no direct quotations or references to the magazine article itself, "which, as it were, does not exist." Murray added, "This is no way to carry on theological argument. However, that's the way it is. Even so, no one is forbidden to make friendly gestures." Nothing came of this effort.

Nor did anything come of a later attempt by Murray to get a new article published in *Civiltà Cattolica,* the Jesuit magazine in Rome. In this work, he explained to McCormick, he discussed the First Amendment of the U.S. Constitution without impugning or referring to the old Catholic Thesis-Hypothesis hornets' nest. Replied McCormick, "I am afraid you do not know that Rome of today. I very seriously doubt that there would be any chance of the *Civiltà* accepting an article by you on the subject of Church-State relations. No; we must be patient; some people never forget.... Deepen and clarify your position, and be ready with your solution ... when the opportune time comes. That is not coming in the present Roman atmosphere." McCormick's letter was dated August 5, 1958. Exactly two months later the Roman atmosphere changed.

"WE HOLD THESE TRUTHS"

The death of Pope Pius XII in October of 1958 and the subsequent election of Pope John XXIII had an immediate, liberating effect on John Courtney Murray. There is no indication that the censure of him and his writings was formally lifted by the Holy Office, but he began to operate as if it did not exist. Pope John created an atmosphere, he later wrote, "in which a lot of things came unstuck — old patterns of thought, behavior, feeling. They were not challenged or refuted, but rather just dropped."[13]

In early 1959 he put together many of his writings on human freedom and the American experience and began negotiations with the Sheed & Ward publishing house for a book. Meanwhile, Murray was contacted by aides of presidential candidate John F. Kennedy, who wondered if Murray's reinterpretation of Catholic church-state doctrine might defray the anti-Catholic bias that was sure to appear against Kennedy, a Catholic, in the 1960 campaign. Murray was happy to cooperate, and his work proved critical during the hot, highly publicized battle. His single greatest contribution may have been the advice he gave in preparation for Kennedy's speech on his Catholicism to the less-than-sympathetic Houston Ministerial Association just two months before the election. Kennedy aide Theodore Sorenson said that he read the final text to Murray on the phone, and Murray added some last-minute suggestions and changes. The speech, described by Sorenson as the "best" of the campaign and "one of the most important of [Kennedy's] life," had the immediate effect of defusing non-Catholic fears without the candidate having to renounce any Catholic convictions.

At about the same time, Murray's book *We Hold These Truths: Catholic Reflections on the American Proposition* was published by Sheed & Ward. In light of the campaign it became a national best seller, further alleviating Protestant fears about a Catholic in the White House. Murray's portrait made the cover of *Time* magazine, which provided an upbeat, popular summary of his theories. Only one reviewer of the book was appalled, and that, predictably, was the intrepid Joseph Fenton. He accused Murray of being careless, showing undisguised sympathy toward liberalism, and contradicting the clear doctrines of Popes Leo XIII and Pius XII.

Murray was not involved in preparations for Pope John's Second Vatican Council in the early 1960s, even though the issue of religious freedom was high on the agenda. Perhaps the new pope and the new U.S. president favored him, but he remained *persona non grata* with the Roman Curia and the Holy Office. The American expert (*peritus*) on church-state issues summoned to Rome by Cardinal Ottaviani was Fenton. Murray, along with several other theologians of note, was especially "disinvited" from the conciliar planning commissions. When asked if he felt bad about the snub, Murray told a friend, "I do. A man doesn't live long, and when something this big is going on, a man feels that he ought to be there."

THE MAIN EVENT

Murray was, however, to be drawn into the council activities from a distance. When Archbishop Lawrence Shehan of Baltimore viewed the proposed drafts on religious freedom prepared by the Curia, he was alarmed and sent Murray copies seeking his suggestions. Murray replied that it appeared certain that Ottaviani's Catholic Thesis theory "will remain on the books, untouched as the essential and pure Catholic doctrine. And the council's 'practical' statements will look like sheer concessions to 'today's circumstances' — a matter of expediency, or, in a word, the thing called 'hypothesis.' ... For my part I think the only practical and realistic thing to do is to join frank issue with the curial Right on the issue of theory. It would not be difficult to do. Few seem to realize how dreadfully weak their position is.... We have a heaven-sent opportunity to effect a genuine development of doctrine in this matter—an absolutely necessary development and one that can quite readily be effected."[14]

Shehan and other bishops heeded his advice, and during the first session of Vatican II a kind of impasse was reached on religious liberty, with Cardinal Ottaviani and the Curia proposing the traditional model, and a growing coterie of bishops from America and Europe pressing for a more liberal interpretation. Seeking to muzzle this drift, Ottaviani succeeded, through the U.S. apostolic delegate, in preventing Murray and other theologians from speaking on conciliar issues at the Catholic University of America during the break between council sessions in early 1963. The strategy backfired because it aroused the patriotism of New York Cardinal Francis Spellman, normally a doctrinal conservative. The powerful and influential Spellman insisted that Murray be designated an official *peritus* to the American bishops, and he would countenance no objections from the Curia.

In Rome during the council's second session in late 1963, Murray got the opportunity he had only dreamt about. Speaking on religious liberty to the full Commission on Faith and Morals—with Ottaviani and Fenton facing him at the end of the table—he called the Catholic Thesis doctrine outmoded, obsolete, and unworkable in the modern world. His position was endorsed in the commission by an eighteen-to-five vote. "A glorious victory for the Good Guys," wrote Murray, in a rare display of exultation. "We had a big party at the Hilton," and "a feeling of euphoria" swept over the bishops and *periti.* At Spellman's request, Murray wrote the speech that the cardinal delivered on religious liberty before the full council. In it, he pounded away on the themes that all people are endowed by their creator with certain inalienable rights and that "the functions of government and law are limited to temporal and terrestrial affairs."

Fenton realized that the tide of battle was turning, and he struggled to uphold the tradition. "Cardinal Ottaviani has not been hoodwinked into imagining that any good is going to come to the Church of God if it passes over some of its dogmas in silence so as to please those who dislike the unchanging continuity of Christ's teaching," he wrote. Those seeking change he labeled "Reformers and Modernists." Fenton would continue for less than a year as editor of the *American Ecclesiastical Review* before giving up the helm after twenty-five years.

In January of 1964 Murray was stricken with acute cardiac arrest and lay in the hospital for several weeks. He had scarcely recovered, two months later, when his superior passed on to him a letter from Archbishop Egidio Vagnozzi, the apostolic delegate in Washington, D.C., apparently in response to an article about the council that Murray had written for *America*. Vagnozzi warned that *periti* "are forbidden to organize currents of opinion or ideas, to hold interviews, or to defend publicly their personal ideas about the council." Murray, feeling perhaps confident for the first time in more than ten years, replied hotly, "What business is this of the Apostolic Delegate? He is in no sense an official of the Council. He has no jurisdiction whatever over the activities of the periti."

THE COUNCIL SPEAKS

During the council's third session, later in 1964, Murray was a veritable whirlwind, conferring and consulting with bishops and assisting on the wording for the final draft of the Declaration on Religious Liberty. He worked especially with Archbishop Karl Alter of Cincinnati on the tricky task of explaining tradition without offending either conservatives or liberals. A particularly sticky point was wording that would not utterly deflate the Spanish hierarchy, which still considered their tight, church-state alliance an ideal for all time. He helped Bishop Ernest Primeau in his council presentation on freedom of conscience, Archbishop Shehan on the biblical foundations of religious liberty, and Archbishop John Carberry of St. Louis on the limits of government in religious affairs. Before the official debate on the declaration in September, Murray briefed all the American bishops at Rome's North American College.

The debate proceeded until October, when, unexpectedly, the council's secretary-general announced the appointment of a new committee to reexamine and revise the declaration. Cardinal Ottaviani had not given up. The overwhelming majority on this committee, including Irish Cardinal Michael Browne, was strongly opposed to new notions of religious liberty. Their proposed revisions, submitted in November, considerably weakened the document, so that further discussion was necessary. The council president announced that the vote would have to be delayed until the fourth session of Vatican II, scheduled to begin in nine months. Those committed to change were dejected at what seemed an obvious stalling tactic by the Curia; Murray called the day of the announcement a "Day of Wrath."[15] No doubt, he realized that his own time was running out. Another heart attack struck, one week after the close of the third session.

Again he came back, using the interim between sessions to persuade hardline traditionalists to change their minds. In a letter to Cardinal Browne, he wrote, "There is an old folk-ballad among us about a boy who was treed by a bear. . . . The refrain runs thus: 'O Lord, if you can't help me, for heaven's sake don't help the bear.' It comes to mind as an expression of my hope in this matter: if your Eminence does not find it possible, in conscience, to come out in favor of the schema, I hope that you will not find it necessary, in conscience, to come out against it." In September of 1965, when the council got underway again, religious liberty was the first agenda item. The American bishops spoke enthusiastically in favor of the text, most of whose ambiguities had been corrected. There were still a few murmurs of opposition. One bishop reportedly interjected, "The voices are the voices of United States bishops, but the thoughts are the thoughts of John Courtney Murray." Murray suffered a collapsed lung in mid-October and was out of action for several weeks. In his absence, the conservative forces made last-ditch attempts to weaken the text and succeeded in a few instances. "In all likelihood," wrote biographer Pelotte, "many of the last-minute changes would never have been made had Murray not been ill."[16]

Murray was there, however, on the fateful day when the final vote on the declaration came before the full assembly. It was a landslide: 2,308 in favor, 70 opposed, and 8 invalid votes. The text echoed Murray's thinking and, indeed, his words in countless places:

- This Vatican synod declares that the human person has a right to religious freedom. This freedom means that all . . . are to be immune from coercion on the part of individuals or of social groups and of any human power, in such wise that . . . no one is to be forced to act in a manner contrary to his own beliefs. Nor is anyone to be restrained from acting in accordance with his own beliefs . . . within due limits.

- Religious bodies have the right not to be hindered in their public teaching and witness to their faith, whether by the spoken or by the written word. . . . [E]veryone ought at all times to refrain from a manner of action which might seem to carry a hint of coercion.

- God calls men to serve Him in spirit and truth. Hence they are bound in conscience but they stand under no compulsion. God has regard for the dignity of the human person whom He Himself created; man is to be guided by his own judgment and he is to enjoy freedom.

- If, in view of peculiar circumstances . . . among certain peoples, special legal recognition is given in the constitutional order of society to one religious body, it is at the same time imperative that the right of all citizens and religious bodies to religious freedom should be recognized and made effective in practice.[17]

"THE PROCESS IS NEVER COMPLETE"

After the postconciliar celebration in Rome — the Mass with Pope Paul, the calls, and the telegrams — Murray returned to the United States. He was soon named director of the John LaFarge Institute in New York City, a Jesuit-sponsored think tank that consulted experts on a wide range of problems, including war, racial inequality, abortion, and world overpopulation. He also became involved in a Church-related commission on conscientious objection (a hot topic during the widening Vietnam War) and in the Lutheran-Catholic ecumenical dialogue. He declined to write a history of the Declaration on Religious Liberty, telling a friend, "I am frankly tired of the whole subject."[18] But in an article, which was published only after his death, he summed up his own ideas on freedom. "In order to be free a man or a society must undergo a process of liberation," he said. "The process is never complete, and it is always precarious, subject to deflection or defeat."

The possession of freedom comes, he said, only from "an arduous education," from learning through experience in this world; "those who haven't learned must blame only themselves; they have been absent from class, truants from the school of history." Society, he noted, is moving slowly and painfully "toward its rightful autonomy — that is its proper secularity." And he regretted that the Church on so many occasions had not endorsed that movement: "On the contrary, it has opposed man's historical movement toward freedom."[19]

His death in August of 1967 elicited a mass of tributes from leaders of countless churches and states. President Lyndon Johnson said that Murray's life transcended the barriers of nation and creed. And Pope Paul VI, through an intermediary, called Murray one "who never stinted in his service to God, the Church, and the Society of Jesus. His humble yet precious theological contributions will be his monument and guide to others."[20]

At Murray's funeral Mass in New York City, friend and longtime associate Fr. Walter J. Burghardt, S.J., said, "Unborn millions will never know how much their freedom is tied to this man whose pen was a powerful protest, a dramatic march, against injustice and inequality, whose research peaked and terminated in the ringing affirmation of an ecumenical council: The right to religious freedom has its foundations not in the Church, not in society or state, not even in objective truth, but 'in the dignity of the human person.'"

TWO

GALILEO

The Earth Moves

In the Louvre in Paris there is a painting by artist Robert Fleury entitled *Galileo.* The seventeenth-century scientist is standing in the great hall of the palace of the Holy Office of the Inquisition. His right fist is held to his chest in a kind of *mea culpa* gesture, and his left hand is spread out over the pages of an open book on a stand, as if he means to push the words out of his sight. Four other volumes are strewn on the floor. Before him, attired in formal, flowing robes, is the commissary general of the Inquisition; behind him, a helmeted guard fingers his sword; in the background, at a long table, the members of the Inquisition, bearded cardinals in birettas, lean forward to hear what the man is saying. But Galileo is not looking at the inquisitor, the guard, the gallery, or the books. He is looking out — out at the viewers of the painting, as if to say, "You, generations to come, will you learn anything from what is happening here?"

Galileo Galilei is perhaps the best-known dissenter in the history of the Church, the central figure in countless books and articles about his ideas and the peculiar circumstances that led him to formally reject in his old age the conclusions he had reached through years of careful, painstaking observation.

His dissent created a firestorm because, unlike so many others that concern only various interpretations of religious doctrine, Galileo's dissent involved a direct confrontation between doctrine and science — and this at the very moment when natural science was beginning to stand on its own feet and assert its own prerogatives. Indeed, Galileo, considered by many the "Father of Modern Science," is most often seen as the winner in his dispute with the Inquisition. And the Church even today still struggles against a nagging reputation as an enemy of science and oppressor of intellectual innovators. Despite these differences, Galileo is very much in the tradition of other responsible dissenters: those who tried to open questions that appeared to have been settled long ago, who sought to do so without contradicting the foundations of religious faith, and who in the process made sacrifices. In the end, it is clear, Galileo made a public sacrifice of his convictions rather than force the issue to an even more embarrassing and tragic conclusion than the one that occurred.

There are some historians who would still deny him the title of responsible dissident. His brilliance was tinged with vanity, ambition, and a penchant for disputes with colleagues, they claim; he exceeded the boundaries of his specialty; he had difficulty in deferring to his spiritual superiors. Still, there are two facts about which no dispute is possible: first, on the scientific issue, Galileo was overwhelmingly correct and the institutional Church was wrong; second, by seeking to quell an idea whose time had come, Church leaders dealt the institutional Church a severe blow from which it is still recovering. This is how it happened.

A DANGEROUS DISCOVERY

On a fateful day in the year 1609, Galileo, a distinguished, forty-three-year-old professor of mathematics and astronomy at the University of Padua in Italy, looked into a twenty-power telescope he had built with his own hands and saw amazing things. He observed a little contingent of "new stars" circling the planet Jupiter (which he came to realize were the planet's moons); he saw that Venus appeared to be turning regularly on its own axis and moving around the sun, not around the earth; that Saturn had "ears" (later identified as rings); that the sun had spots that moved so as to indicate that it rotated on its own axis; that comets appeared and disappeared in the night sky. All this disputed the conventional wisdom of the ages. For centuries, it was commonly believed that the earth was the center of the universe, that it stood still while all the heavenly bodies — sun, moon, stars — circled around it every twenty-four hours, causing day and night.

This earth-centered model had been challenged occasionally, but in the absence of confirming evidence, what seemed apparent was regarded as real. As far as the Catholic Church was concerned, the scientific authority on this was the ancient philosopher Aristotle, who viewed the earth as a changing, imperfect, unmoving body surrounded by forty-nine perfectly shaped, unchangeable spheres rotating in perfect circles around the earth. His ideas seemed compatible with both Scripture and the testimony of the Church Fathers.

The telescope was a quite recent invention, and even though some purists called it a device of the devil because it gave unnatural power to the human eye, scientists were using it and making notations. It required little time for Galileo to sense the implications of what he saw through his small telescope.

He was fully aware of the controversial conclusions of Nicholas Copernicus, a Polish astronomer who died twenty-three years before Galileo's birth. Basing his conclusions solely on mathematics and the limited astronomy of his day, Copernicus described a sun-centered (heliocentric) model in which the earth and other planets rotated on their own axes and also moved in orbits around the sun, which remained still, at least in relation to the movement of its planets. Copernicus knew that his interpretation conflicted with the Church's earth-centered (geocentric) concept. Thus, he did not allow publication of his work in book form until he was near death; and for good measure, he included a preface (the authorship of which remains in dispute) that claimed that his heliocentric model should be seen as "hypothetic" only, simply a device for calculating the position of planets and not a challenge to any Church belief.

Some consternation arose over Copernicus's book, but the issue really came alive when Galileo published his own small book, *The Starry Messenger,* in 1610, and a second volume, *The Sunspot Letters,* the following year. Without openly contradicting authority, Galileo presented his findings, all of which confirmed Copernicus's theory of a rotating and moving earth and a relatively still sun. Tracts immediately appeared castigating the books' discrepancies with Aristotle, some even detecting the whiff of heresy in the conclusions. Much of this was to be expected. These scientific rumblings were occurring just thirty years after the Council of Trent had finished its efforts to put a lid on Protestant heresies and set the Church on a more even, less turbulent course.

Galileo remained confident for a time. He was, after all, a believing Catholic with two daughters who had become nuns; he was a personal friend of Cardinal Maffeo Barberini (destined to become the next pope, Urban VIII); he was on intimate terms with the influential duke of Tuscany (his place of birth); and he had just been invited into the newly formed Lincean Academy, the world's first scientific society. Besides, Copernicus's book had so far survived scrutiny, and Galileo was also careful to couch his ideas as suppositions and hypotheses to be discussed and judged by competent authorities.

Nevertheless, the criticism mounted and colleagues warned him that the Vatican was becoming restless, especially after a Dominican priest in 1614 filed charges with the Office of the Inquisition. Galileo attempted to respond to inquirers through long letters, which were widely circulated and which then became themselves the source of further discussion and controversy. Somewhat contradictory rumors emanated from Rome. Cardinal Robert Bellarmine, a consultant to the Inquisition and perhaps the most influential churchman of the era, said at one point that he believed Galileo was following a prudent course by "speaking suppositionally and not absolutely." He then added that to maintain that the sun-centered model actually corresponds to reality would be a "very dangerous thing, likely not only to irritate all scholastic philosophers and theologians, but also to harm the Holy Faith by rendering Holy Scripture false."[1]

CAN THE FATHERS ERR?

The argument from Scripture for an earth-centered system was founded on a very literal interpretation of several Old Testament texts. The sun's apparent movement in relation to the earth could be inferred from Psalm 19:4–6, which says, "the sun comes forth like a groom from his bridal chamber and...joyfully runs its course," or from Ecclesiastes 1:5: "the sun rises, the sun sets; then to its place it speeds and there it rises [again]"; or from Joshua 10:12–13: "Joshua declared, 'Sun, stand still over Gibeon, and, Moon, you also, over the Vale of Aijalon.' And the sun stood still, and the moon halted till the people had vengeance on their enemies." The earth's immovability seemed clear from Psalm 104:5: "You fixed the earth on its foundations, unshakeable for ever and ever."

Galileo believed that if the discussion were to go forward, it would be helpful to examine the Bible in a less mechanistic way. In this effort he showed a grasp of Scripture that was far ahead of his time — too far ahead, as it turned out. In a long letter to a friendly inquirer, he wrote,

> Though the Scripture cannot err, nevertheless some of its inter-preters and expositors can sometimes err in various ways. One of these would be very serious and very frequent, namely to want to limit oneself always to the literal meaning of the words.... It would seem to me that in disputes about natural phenomena, it [Scripture] should be reserved to the last place. For the Holy Scripture and nature both equally derive from the divine Word, the former as the dictation of the Holy Spirit, the latter as the most obedient executor of God's commands; moreover in order to adapt itself to the understanding of all people, it was appro-priate for the Scripture to say many things which are different from absolute truth, in appearance and in regard to the meaning of words.... I think it would be prudent not to allow anyone to oblige scriptural passages to have to maintain the truth of any physical conclusions whose contrary could ever be proved to us by the senses.[2]

Similarly in his correspondence, Galileo tried to propose a more fluid, less rigid way of understanding tradition — an approach that was also far ahead of its time. It was generally true, he conceded, that where the Fathers of the Church were unanimous on a belief, it should be regarded as an article of faith. And it was perfectly clear that none of the Fathers ever contradicted the proposition that the earth was still and the sun moved around it. Galileo then offered a fascinating insight:

I should think that at most this ought to apply only to those conclusions which the Fathers discussed and inspected with great diligence and debated on both sides of the issue.... However, the earth's rest and the sun's motion are not of this sort, given that in those times this opinion [that the earth circled the sun] was...far from academic dispute and was not examined.... Thus one may believe that the Fathers did not even think of discussing it since the scriptural passages, their own opinion, and popular consensus were all in agreement.... Therefore, it is not enough to say that all the Fathers accept the earth's rest, etc., and so it is an article of faith; rather, one would have to prove that they condemned the contrary opinion.... Their failure to reflect upon it and discuss it made them leave it stand as the current opinion, but not as something resolved and established.[3]

"FOOLISH AND ABSURD" PROPOSITIONS

Such subtleties made little impression in Rome, because the juridical process was already in motion. In late 1615 it was announced that the Inquisition would examine *The Sunspot Letters* for heresy. Eleven consultants, all theologians, finished their work the following February but did not speak specifically about either Galileo's or Copernicus's writings. Instead, they responded to two "propositions" without attributing them to any author. They found the first, which said, "The sun is the center of the world and completely devoid of local motion," to be "foolish and absurd...and formally heretical since it explicitly contradicts in many places the sense of Holy Scripture, according to the literal meaning of the word." The second, which stated, "The earth is not the center of the world, nor motionless, but it moves as a whole," was declared both absurd and "erroneous in faith."[4] These findings were immediately endorsed by Pope Paul V.

Under orders from the pope, Bellarmine summoned Galileo and read to him the declarations of the commission. From this, Galileo concluded that he must tread lightly in any future claims, but he apparently believed that he was still free to write about the Copernican concept of the universe as long as he treated it strictly as a mathematical hypothesis. (However, as will be discussed below, there is considerable uncertainty surrounding exactly what occurred at this meeting.)

Immediately, reports began to circulate claiming that Galileo had been expressly ordered by the great Bellarmine to cease any further discussion of the sun-centered model altogether. So Galileo approached the cardinal seeking clarification and obtained from him a signed certificate asserting that he had not been required to renounce under oath or in any other way his opinions, and that he had merely been informed that the Copernican theory could not be portrayed as physical fact, due to its conflict with the Scriptures. Galileo felt reassured, and after a personal meeting with Pope Paul, he was further reassured; he quickly set to work on an extensive presentation of his research. Other developments in the next few years were also encouraging. Though the book of Copernicus had been placed on the Index of Forbidden Books just after the 1616 Inquisition report, it was removed from the list four years later when alterations of the text clarified its exclusively hypothetical intent. Then in 1623 Galileo's friend Barberini was elected pope as Urban VIII, and the new pontiff began having regular weekly meetings with the scientist, expressing genuine interest in his work.

A CHANGE OF SEASON

In 1630, fourteen years after his first encounter with the Inquisition, Galileo finally finished his magnum opus, *A Dialogue on Two Great World Systems,* and immediately sought an imprimatur (permission to publish) from the Roman censor. There followed a series of delays and strange complications, which greatly frustrated Galileo. The censor sought and finally obtained a second opinion approving of the book but then began to pass it on to the intended publisher slowly, page by page. Then the publisher died and a new one had to be sought. This, along with an outbreak of the plague, further held up the work. Finally, in 1623, two years after completion, the book received a rather unique imprimatur, in part from the censor in Rome and in part from the censor in Florence.

In the introduction to the *Dialogue,* Galileo explained that he gave the better arguments to the Copernican belief that the world travels around the sun and not vice versa in order to show the academic world that Rome is not ignorant or closed-minded on matters of modern science and that "from these parts emerge not only dogmas for the salvation of the soul, but also ingenious discoveries for the delight of the mind." Still, he noted, all this was to be regarded as mathematical hypothesis only. To assert Copernican conclusions as fact, he said, would be contrary to "piety, religion, acknowledgement of divine omnipotence, and awareness of the weakness of the human mind."[5]

The book was structured as a debate between three imaginary spokesmen: Salviati, who held the Copernican-Galilean position; Simplicio, representing the traditional Aristotelian, earth-centered approach; and Sagredi, a kind of impartial host, referee, and asker of intelligent questions. In the conclusion, Galileo had Salviati reiterate for good measure the hypothetical nature of his position by saying, "These ideas are novel, my mind is imperfect, the subject is a great one, and finally I do not ask and have not asked from others an assent which I myself do not give to this fancy; I could very easily regard it as a most unreal chimera and a most solemn paradox." It was also agreed that the final words of the discussion be the very ones that Urban VIII often used when asked about the Church's stance on the new science: "It would be excessively bold if someone should want to limit and compel divine power and wisdom to a particular fancy of his."[6]

Here Galileo made a great strategic blunder, because he put these words in the mouth of Simplicio (a name that could be easily translated "simpleton"), whose relatively weak defense of the time-honored earth-centered supposition had been continually refuted by Salviati's wise insights and explanations.

A Dialogue on Two Great World Systems attained an immediate, wide circulation, only to be suddenly barred by order of the pope himself. Unprepared for such a reaction, Galileo was stunned; almost overnight his old friend had become his fiercest opponent.

The reasons for the switch have been discussed and debated. It seemed to many readers of the book that Galileo had done too good a job in presenting the sun-centered model; readers could see through the book's disclaimers and grasp the scientific logic of Salviati's arguments behind the hypothetical veneer. Urban felt betrayed; he had expected that Church approval would be obtained solely in Rome and not shared with Florence; and he was furious that his well-known words had been attributed in the book to the hapless Simplicio. Furthermore, the *Dialogue* appeared just when the pope was in the midst of a public relations disaster. The Holy Roman emperor had suffered a severe defeat against an army headed by the Swedish Protestant Gustavus Adolphus, and many were blaming Urban for not providing needed support to the Catholic side. He was therefore seeking to demonstrate his authority and his fidelity to the Catholic values in the face of opposition. Galileo was a likely target of opportunity.

Whatever the motivation, Urban moved decisively against his one-time associate, appointing a special commission, a kind of grand jury, to determine possible charges for the Office of the Inquisition. Following a meeting with the pope, the Tuscan ambassador to the Holy See told Galileo's longtime supporter, the duke of Tuscany, that "the sky is about to fall." Urban, he said, "exploded into great anger" during the discussion, "and suddenly he told me that even our Galilei had dared enter where he should not have, into the most serious and dangerous subjects which could be stirred up at this time." When the ambassador suggested that Galileo deserved to know in advance the nature of the charges against him, the pope allegedly replied, "The Holy Office does not proceed in this way. . . . These things are never given in advance. . . . Such is not the custom." He then told the ambassador that he had "appointed a Commission of theologians and other persons versed in various sciences, serious and of holy mind, who are weighing every minutia, word for word, since one is dealing with the most perverse subject one could ever come across."[7]

The commission determined that the book provided more than ample probable cause for formal charges of heresy. Wrote one of the members,

> If he [Galileo] had undertaken this discussion only with the purpose of engaging in a disputation and exercising of the mind, he would not have waged such arrogant war against . . . Aristotelians, nor would he have ridiculed Aristotle and his followers so insolently. . . . He should have posited the earth's motion as something he intended to analyze deductively, not as something to be proved

by destroying the opposite view, as indeed he does in the entire work.... He declares war on everybody and regards as dwarfs all who are not...Copernican.[8]

Galileo at this time, in 1633, was seventy years old and in declining health. He was gradually losing his eyesight, had severe arthritis, and suffered from bouts of colitis. When summoned to Rome for trial, he sought to have the proceedings moved to Florence. This was denied, and he agreed to come to Rome after officers of the Inquisition threatened to transport him there in chains.

FORCED TO RECANT

When the formal proceedings finally began, Galileo believed that he could defend himself adequately. He still had in his possession the signed certificate that Cardinal Bellarmine had given him seventeen years before, in 1616. Bellarmine had since died, but the document said that Galileo had not been told to retract his views or to cease writing about his discoveries; he had simply been informed that such views could not be presented as absolute fact.

However, the questioning had hardly begun when his defenses were breached. The prosecutors presented him with a copy of a "special injunction" dated 1616, which utterly contradicted the Bellarmine certificate. It stated that the cardinal explicitly told Galileo that "his opinion was erroneous and he should abandon it...and was henceforth not to hold, teach or defend it in any way whatever [as fact or hypothesis] either orally or in writing; otherwise the Holy Office would start proceedings against him." It continued, "The same Galileo acquiesced in this injunction and promised to obey."[9]

Why, asked his inquisitors, had he disobeyed this order and failed to inform the censors of his book about the existence of the injunction? Galileo insisted that he had neither seen nor heard of this document, which bore no signature, until the moment it was handed to him, and that he had no memory of ever agreeing to such stipulations. (No explanation has ever been provided about the authenticity or source of the injunction, and some scholars contend that it was a forgery explicitly designed to trump the Bellarmine certificate.)

The commissary general of the Inquisition then met privately with Galileo, who was reeling from the implications of this new evidence, and he reported real progress. "By the grace of the Lord, I accomplished my purpose," he wrote. "I made him grasp his error…and that he had gone too far in his book; he expressed everything with heartfelt words…and was ready for a judicial confession."[10]

Galileo was given time to reread the *Dialogue* text and was urged — after being shown the instruments of torture — to say whatever he wished in an official deposition. He wrote, "If I had to write out the same arguments now, there is no doubt I would weaken them in such a way that they could not appear to exhibit a force which they really and essentially lack. My error was, and I confess it, one of vain ambition, pure ignorance and inadvertence." He did not intend to deceive, he insisted, nor had he presented the case for the earth's rotation "through cunning or an insincere intention."[11]

Such an admission was not sufficient for the prosecutors. They insisted that he was aware of the injunction and chose to ignore it. The more important issue before the court was this: Does Galileo himself now hold the condemned proposition that the earth moves and in fact orbits around the sun? When the question was posed he responded, "I do not hold this opinion of Copernicus, and I have not held it after being ordered by the injunction to abandon it. For the rest, here I am in your hands; do as you please."[12]

After conferring, the ten cardinal members of the Inquisition gathered in the great hall and presented their verdict, which was signed by seven, with three abstaining:

We say, pronounce, sentence and declare that you, the above-mentioned Galileo because of the things deduced in the trial and confessed by you, have rendered yourself according to this Holy Office vehemently suspected of heresy, namely of having held and believed a doctrine which is false and contrary to the divine and Holy Scripture; that the sun is the center of the world and does not move from east to west, and that the earth moves and is not the center of the world, and that one may hold and defend as probable an opinion after it has been declared and defined contrary to Holy Scripture.[13]

So that "this serious and pernicious error not remain completely unpunished...and as an example to others," Galileo was sentenced to formal imprisonment in the Office of the Inquisition "at our pleasure," and was required to recite the seven penitential psalms once a week for the next three years.

The verdict, "vehemently suspected of heresy," requires some explanation. According to Galileo scholar James Orgren, the suspicion did not relate to the "matter" of the act. Galileo was in fact found guilty of heresy, an act considered intrinsically evil. The term "vehemence" measured the degree of evil or malicious intent in the heretical position. If he actually had been found guilty of vehement or formal heresy, he could have been sentenced to death by fire or at least to lifetime imprisonment. The court showed some mercy, therefore, in finding him only "suspected" of evil intention.[14]

On his knees before the court, Galileo was required to read a lengthy abjuration of his position, which said in part:

> After having been notified that this doctrine is contrary to Holy Scripture, I wrote and published a book in which I treat of this already condemned doctrine and adduce very effective reasons in its favor, without refuting them in any way....Desiring to remove from the minds of Your Eminences and every faithful Christian this vehement suspicion rightly conceived against me...I abjure, curse, and detest the above-mentioned errors and heresies and in general each and every other error, heresy, and sect contrary to the Holy Church.[15]

"We will never know," writes Orgren, "what transpired that day in Galileo's heart. Did he capitulate out of fear for his life? If so, mortal or immortal? Was he concerned about scandalizing the faithful? Did he consider that to play the hero might have wounded his beloved Church more than his capitulation? Was it a combination of all these, or more? To these questions, Galileo, the answer man, left us without answers."[16]

A CHASM BETWEEN RELIGION AND SCIENCE

His public life was finished, and Galileo remained in a state of shock for several months. Pope Urban, his rage spent, quickly allowed the repentant heretic to depart from the bleak accommodations of the Inquisition in Rome and take up house arrest — under stringent conditions — first in Siena and a few months later in a villa in his native Tuscany. Galileo's friends and supporters were devastated by the verdict, none more so than his older daughter, Maria Celeste, a nun thirty-three years of age. "The news of your fresh trouble has pierced my soul with grief," she wrote a few weeks after the trial. Nine months later she was dead.

"I was very fond of them [his two daughters in the convent]," Galileo wrote to a friend, "especially the elder, who possessed extraordinary mental gifts combined with rare goodness of heart; and she was very much attached to me." The apparent cause of death was a "profound melancholy" that gripped her during her father's sufferings and severely undermined her health. In his sorrow, Galileo wrote, "I hear her constantly calling me," and he spoke often of his own approaching death.[17]

His spirit, however, refused to be crushed, even under such an avalanche. With encouragement from his son, and with the assistance of a few young scientists, he began studying and writing again, achieving amazing productivity in the nine years of life that remained. He was, of course, strictly forbidden to touch again any matters involving the heavenly bodies, so he turned his attention to the more abstract principles of physical motion, a subject he had been researching even before he first looked into the telescope. His new work in this area, published in 1636 as *A Dialogue on the New Sciences,* had a particularly ironic effect. Galileo's principles would in time be taken up and developed by Isaac Newton (who was born the year Galileo died); they would be published in Newton's own book *Principia,* to establish conclusively that the earth, sun, and other bodies do indeed move, and that it is the sun that rests, as Copernicus and Galileo had tried to demonstrate, Scripture and tradition notwithstanding.

When at last he rested, in 1642, a public funeral was planned in Tuscany, and a marble monument was prepared. But officials in Rome ruled such honors "inappropriate" for someone "who had aroused the greatest scandal in all Christendom."[18] Galileo's remains would thus be hidden away for ninety-five years, until his body was moved with great ceremony to a church mausoleum in Tuscany. Twenty years after that, in 1757, when the fundamental accuracy of his research had been established beyond reasonable doubt, the Congregation of the Index removed its blanket ban on all books that taught that the earth moves — except those by Copernicus, Galileo, and Kepler. Another sixty-five years would pass before the works of these three scientists were removed from the Index.

The silencing of Galileo had a lasting ripple effect all over Europe. He had most certainly been made an example to those who presumed to study science in regions where the Catholic Church was strong and exercised its authority. As a result, notes Orgren, "the Catholic countries like Italy and France lost their chance to significantly influence the process we call the Scientific Revolution."[19] It was left to Newton in England and others in Protestant countries to explore new realms and propose innovative theories. However, with fallout from the Galileo affair still penetrating all of society, this unshackled search for truth was frequently accompanied by hostility to spiritual and religious truth. Science and religion, once separate but compatible areas of inquiry, came to be regarded as bitter enemies.

A similar separation — one that continues today — occurred in philosophy. According to Jerome Langford, a Galileo scholar,

> For all practical purposes, science and speculative philosophy [became] unrelated, completely divorced. This situation had serious consequences.... The separation ... has left a gap between technical know-how and the priorities which should govern the use of that knowledge. Unless science is related to values, the whole of human life must suffer.[20]

In short, the repression of Galileo's dissent precipitated a great chasm between religion and secular knowledge that remains unbridged.

Was anything learned? It is the question that Galileo seems still to be asking from his place on the wall in the Louvre. Yes, said Pope John Paul II, when in 1992, four hundred years after Galileo's condemnation, he acknowledged that the Church erred. "Galileo had to suffer a great deal at the hands of men and organisms of the Church," he said, calling the unfortunate incident the product of "a tragic mutual incomprehension." Thanks in part to Galileo, who "formulated important norms of an epistemological character which are indispensable to reconcile Scripture and science," John Paul explained, the Church no longer believes that Scripture in its "literal sense" can be used to explain the physical world.[21] He was referring, obviously, to the letters Galileo wrote early in the dispute, warning that Scripture should not be forced to say more than it intended to say and suggesting that scientific discoveries might aid in determining what the Bible is really trying to teach. Pope John Paul did not expressly acknowledge Galileo's other contribution: his perception that what we regard as a fixed, uninterrupted tradition may under scrutiny turn out to be a culturally based assumption that had never been questioned or even subjected to serious discussion. That is an area that Church historians and theologians are only now beginning to explore.

The pope returned again to Galileo in his 1998 encyclical, *Fides et ratio,* citing with approval the scientist's claim that the truths of faith and science cannot be in contradiction, since both come equally from the same divine source. There is, of course, some irony here, since Galileo's contention on this point was granted not a shred of consideration during his trial in the seventeenth century.

Yet *Fides et ratio* suggests that something has indeed been learned. The encyclical itself is a massive, thirty-five-thousand-word work in preparation for twelve years, whose major goal is to establish the existence of a "profound and indissoluble union between the knowledge of reason and the knowledge of faith. . . . The unity of truth is a fundamental premise of human reasoning. . . . It is the one and the same God who establishes and guarantees the intelligibility and reasonableness of the natural order of things upon which scientists confidently depend, and who reveals himself as the Father of our Lord Jesus Christ." Separating faith from reason, said the pope, can only "diminish the capacity of men and women to know themselves, the world, and God in an appropriate way."[22]

JOHN HENRY NEWMAN
A Sense of the Faithful

In 1859 John Henry Newman was fifty-eight years old and somewhat worn from the demands of his celebrity status as the Church's intellectual leader of the age. For two decades he had written almost a book a year, and his correspondence was prodigious. (It is estimated that in his lifetime he wrote upwards of twenty thousand letters to supporters, critics, and friends.) The Newman name, recognized everywhere in England and on the Continent, was always associated with the Oxford Movement, a profound reexamination of the foundations of Christianity by a group of young Anglican thinkers. The Oxford Movement had led him and many others into the Catholic Church during the 1840s.

Newman became convinced that he must convert to Catholicism almost entirely through the study of church history, especially ancient church history, and in particular church history of the fourth and fifth centuries. As an Anglican, he had tried to prove that the Church of England represented in his own day a Middle Way (*Via Media*) between the rigidity of the Roman Church on the one hand and the laxity of much of Protestantism on the other. As such, he argued, Anglicanism seemed the legitimate successor to those Middle Way movements in the early Church that sorted through contentious opinions and arrived at orthodox doctrine. But the more he dug into the clash of old heresies — Arians versus Apollinarians, Nestorians versus Monophysites — the more he became certain that he, as an Anglican, was in the tradition of heresy, not orthodoxy. "Now here in the middle of the fifth century," he wrote, "I found as it seemed to me, the Christendom of the sixteenth and seventeenth centuries reflected. I saw my face in that mirror and I was a Monophysite."[1]

Newman shared his struggles in a series of widely discussed tracts, only to find himself censured by the bishops of the Anglican communion. In 1845 he published much of his research and conclusions in a book, *An Essay on the Development of Christian Doctrine,* whose significance is still much discussed today. He entered the Catholic Church in 1847 and was ordained a priest eighteen months later.

The transition was not easy. While many Anglican associates he left behind railed against his apostasy, many in the English Catholic Church offered less than warm hospitality to these "new Catholics." The intellectual life of the Church was at low ebb at the time. The faithful, generally passive, compliant, and unconcerned about doctrinal matters, accepted without comment an authority structure that, under Pope Pius IX, was becoming more and more centralized. Besides, the Catholic hierarchy preferred that the flock maintain a low profile in a country where Roman Catholicism was still a much resented minority denomination. The tension between the new and old Catholics was to haunt Newman for the rest of his life, but it did little to obstruct his literary and oral output — until the fateful year 1859.

"WHO ARE THE LAITY?"

Newman was just back from Ireland, where he had attempted without much success to establish a Catholic university. On his return he agreed somewhat reluctantly to become editor of a journal called the *Rambler,* whose aim was to bring a measure of scholarship to Catholic thinking. But the magazine's outgoing editors had just rankled England's Catholic hierarchy by arguing against their judgment on a sensitive matter.

The British government had set up a Royal Commission on Elementary Education to find ways to improve the admittedly inferior quality of public schooling throughout the country. The *Rambler* argued that at least one Catholic ought to be on the commission and that the commission members should be invited to visit Catholic as well as public schools to suggest improvements. But the bishops wanted nothing to do with the commission. Surely, persisted the *Rambler,* the views of Catholic parents and teachers deserved consideration before a decision to cooperate was finalized.

Newman's first issue of the magazine, dated May 1859, dutifully presented in full the bishops' position on the subject. Nevertheless, he could not restrain himself from stating a brief opinion in the small-type, unsigned commentary section in the back pages. Wrote Newman,

> We do unfeignedly believe... that their Lordships [the English bishops] really desire to know the opinion of the laity on subjects in which the laity are especially concerned. If even in the preparation of a dogmatic definition the faithful are consulted, as lately in the instance of the Immaculate Conception, it is at least as natural to anticipate such an act of kind feeling and sympathy in great practical questions.[2]

He was referring here to the fact that Pius IX had consulted both the bishops of the world and the theology faculties of major universities before he declared just five years previously the dogma of the Immaculate Conception. The small print notwithstanding, an immediate uproar followed. Newman had no business interjecting himself in the issue, said his critics, and the hierarchy concurred. He was called in by his own bishop, William Ullathorne of Birmingham, and told that he had erred seriously in trying to rouse the laity on a question already decided. The laity are a "peaceable set," said Ullathorne, they have "a deep faith," they do not "like to hear that anyone doubted" episcopal decisions. Newman replied that an absolutely docile laity was not good for the Church. Ullathorne retorted, "Who are the laity?" to which Newman replied, "The Church would look foolish without them."[3]

The bottom line was this, according to Bishop Ullathorne: the next issue of the *Rambler,* July 1859, would be the second and last under Newman's editorship. He accepted the decree, though not without some resentment, and set to work almost immediately preparing the issue.

When it appeared, the issue was not, as usual, a selection of articles by various writers, but one long article by Newman himself, an article of some fifteen thousand words — almost a small book — entitled *On Consulting the Faithful in Matters of Doctrine*. The tremors that followed Newman's remarks in the May *Rambler* were nothing compared to the earthquake precipitated by the July issue. For here he made explicit ideas concerning the nature of the Church that he had been developing in earlier works. In the years to come, *Consulting the Faithful* would be offered as evidence that Newman was a dissident, a disloyal Catholic, the most dangerous man in England, even a heretic. And his career very nearly came to a tragic conclusion.

ARIANISM: A STUBBORN HERESY

In this extended essay, Newman returned to a subject about which he was undoubtedly the world's leading historian: the Arian heresy of the fourth century. He used the dispute over Arianism to contend that the Church is not and never was an absolute monarchy, and that the laity are not passive subjects in the Church but integral actors. This is so, he insisted, not just in carrying the gospel message into the world, but also in the actual formation of Christian doctrine.

The Arians believed that though Jesus was God's son, he was not God himself; rather, he was an extraordinarily lofty creature (the *Logos,* or "Word," as St. John's Gospel says), higher than any human or angel. This conviction spread rapidly through the early Church, especially in the East, but it was officially condemned by a gathering of some three hundred bishops at the city of Nicea in the year 325. That gathering, since recognized as the Church's first ecumenical council, produced the Nicene Creed, still recited now some sixteen hundred years later. "God from God, light from light, true God from true God, begotten not made" — these are not seemingly unnecessary repetitions of the obvious. They are specific repudiations of various Arian formulas, and all were intended to affirm the mysterious doctrine that in Jesus, man and God are truly joined.

Newman then recreated through an examination of historical texts what occurred in the Church for sixty years following the Council of Nicea. Though officially rejected, Arianism thrived. It was preserved and presented as the authentic faith at almost every level of Church and civil authority and in virtually every capital and corner of Christendom. There were a few bishops — and only a few — like Hilary, Basil, and Gregory Nazianzen, who remained faithful to the Nicene doctrine. Athanasius, who also held out against the heresy, was forever memorialized in the phrase "Athanasius against the world."

Newman presented in his essay an exhaustive list of particulars showing the extent of the apparent Arian victory. Some examples:

- The synods of Caesarea, 334, and Tyre, 335, accused Athanasius of rebellion, sedition, tyranny, sacrilege, and magic, deposed him as bishop of Alexandria, and banished him to Gaul.

- At the Council of Arles, 353, all those in attendance, including the pope's legate, were persuaded to subscribe to the Arian doctrine; a lone dissenting bishop was banished.

- At the Council of Milan, 355, more than three hundred bishops confirmed the condemnation of Athanasius and other holdouts.

- In 357 Pope Liberius himself, under pressure from Emperor Constantius, also confirmed the sentence against Athanasius.

- In 363 Jerome declared, "Nearly all the churches in the whole world, under the pretense of peace and the emperor, are polluted with the communion of the Arians."[4]

Why, then, did the Arian heresy not prevail? Newman's answer was the laity. They strenuously and persistently dissented from the doctrine in the face of excommunication, persecution, even martyrdom. He produced copious citations from writings of that troubled period to make his point. Some excerpts:

- In Alexandria, according to Athanasius, the Arian bishops "attacked the holy virgins and brethren with naked swords; they beat with scourges their persons...so that their feet were lamed by the stripes...." At the church of Quirinus "some they slew, some they trampled under foot, others they beat, cast into prison or banished." On the week after Pentecost, "when the people…had gone to the cemetery to pray, because they all refused communion with [the Arian bishop],…a multitude of soldiers proceeded to attack the people" and eventually banished all who would not submit to the Arian belief.

• Elsewhere in Egypt, Emperor Valens issued an edict ordering the banishment of all who accepted the Nicene Creed. "Depopulation and ruin to an immense extent followed; some were dragged before tribunals, others cast into prison, and many tortured."

• At Antioch the Arian bishop concealed his convictions for fear of an "uprising" of the multitude; instead, he withheld priesthood from anyone accepting the Nicene teaching, while ordaining Arian believers and urging them to disseminate the doctrine widely.

• From Edessa came a report of one futile effort to impose Arian doctrine on the citizens. Hearing that Nicene faithful had crowded into a local church, the emperor dispatched soldiers to slay them. As they approached, the captain observed a "poor woman leading her own little child by the hand" toward the church and asked her, "Wretched woman, whither are you running in so disorderly a manner?" She replied, "To the same place that others are hastening." "Have your not heard," said he, "that the [soldiers] are about to put to death all that shall be found there?" "Yes," said the woman, "and therefore I hasten that I also may be found there." "And whither are you dragging that little child?" asked the captain. The woman answered, "That he also may be vouchsafed the honor of martyrdom." The captain was so moved that he reportedly "succeeded in restraining the emperor's wrath."[5]

• In Samasota, according to one account, the Arian bishop, riding one day on his ass, passed some youths on the street. When their ball accidentally rolled beneath the feet of the animal, the youths "uttered loud exclamations believing that the ball was contaminated." They then lit a fire and hurled the ball through it several times in hopes the ball might thereby be purified of any Arian tendencies.

- At Rome, Pope Liberius, who had signed a pro-Arian document, found himself afterwards shunned by the masses; the crowds would not even go to the public baths, lest by accident they be touched by the same water in which Liberius bathed.

Though many details in these accounts sound quite apocryphal, they all witness to a powerful, prevailing antipathy toward Arianism and its adherents.

By the late 370s the Arian cause was losing energy. It was patently evident that the mass of ordinary Christians would not accept a doctrine that made Jesus less than the incarnation of God. And so in 381 the First Council of Constantinople, attended by 150 bishops, solemnly reaffirmed the creed of Nicea. This time the hierarchy, both in the East and West, accepted the decision. Arianism was relegated at last to the footnotes of history.

HERESY TRIUMPHANT!

Newman's conclusion from his lengthy, fourth-century excursion was clear but shocking — and it was just this that got him in trouble. Open, sustained dissent against an overwhelming preponderance of Church authority was, he declared, the very instrument by which an erroneous doctrine had been eradicated and the true tradition vindicated. He summed it up with typical flourish:

> The Nicene dogma was maintained during the greater part of the 4th century...not by the unswerving firmness of the Holy See, Councils or Bishops, but...by the *consensus fidelium* [consent of the faithful]. On the one hand, I say, that there was a temporary suspense of the functions of the *Ecclesia docens* [the teaching church]. The body of the Bishops failed in their confession of the faith. They spoke variously, one against another; there was nothing after Nicea, of firm, unvarying, consistent testimony, for nearly sixty years. There were untrustworthy Councils, unfaithful Bishops; there was weakness, fear of consequences,

misguidance, delusion, hallucination, endless, hopeless, extending itself into nearly every corner of the Catholic church. The
comparatively few who remained faithful were discredited and
driven into exile; the rest were either deceivers or were deceived.[6]

To explain how such a situation could happen — and how it
might happen again — Newman discussed in the essay his own,
well-developed theology of the "sense" and "consent" of the faithful.
Consulting the people is not to be regarded as just a friendly gesture
on the part of pope and bishops, he maintained; consultation is something the laity have a right to expect. Their view may serve at times as
a needed "witness to the truth" of a revealed doctrine. This sense of the
faithful, he said, springs from a sort of instinct for the truth deep in
the bosom of the Mystical Body; it acts as a spiritual antibody rejecting
false teaching, just as the physical body tends to set up barriers against
infection.

Church teaching therefore could not be, in Newman's view, a top-
down, one-way-street enterprise. Instead, it must be a *conspiratio* of the
faithful and their pastors, by which he did not mean "conspiracy" in
the usual, negative sense, but literally a "breathing together," a cooper-
ative venture: the teaching church, before teaching, must discover what
the believing church really believes, so that the believing church "rec-
ognizes" as authentic that which is presented to it as doctrine.[7] Where
the believing church does not recognize teaching (the very situation in
the fourth century), it is clear that the necessary breathing together has
not occurred. The sources of the doctrine, which the teaching church
must discover, are many in Newman's view:

> I think I am right in saying that the tradition of the Apostles,
> committed to the whole Church in its various constituents and
> functions *per modum unius* [through a kind of unity], manifests
> itself variously at various times: sometimes by the mouth of the
> episcopacy, sometimes by the doctors, sometimes by the people,
> sometimes by liturgies, rites, ceremonies, and customs, by events,
> disputes, movements, and all those other phenomena which are
> comprised under the name of history. It follows that none of these
> channels of tradition may be treated with disrespect.[8]

This, he quickly noted, in no way undercuts the authority of the teaching church, which has the responsibility of wading prayerfully and cautiously through this tangle of sources. Yet, added Newman, of all the sources, "I am accustomed to lay stress on the *consensus fidelium*."[9]

In the history of the Arian dispute, he saw an illuminating example of how all this works. At that time, "in order to know the tradition of the Apostles, we must have recourse to the faithful.... Their voice then is the voice of tradition." The Arian situation, he contended, is "as striking an instance" as he could find that the voice of authentic tradition "may express itself in certain cases, not by Councils, nor Fathers, nor Bishops, but by the *communis fidelium sensus* (common sense of the faithful)."[10]

"THE MOST DANGEROUS MAN IN ENGLAND"

Newman had to know (better than anyone alive) that such an aggressive proclamation of the prerogatives of the laity — so much at odds with approved doctrine — would not be casually dismissed. The accepted wisdom in Rome and elsewhere was that the laity's position is by definition a passive one; there were the "teachers" (pope and bishops) and there were the "taught" (laity or nonordained), the latter category constituting the recipients of teaching. This assumption would become considerably more explicit just eleven years after Newman's 1859 bombshell — in the elevation of papal infallibility to dogmatic status at the First Vatican Council.

One of the first to respond to the article was Newman's longtime nemesis, theologian John Gillow. He was particularly scandalized by the claim that there could be a suspense (that is, a suspension) of the functioning of the teaching church, since, he insisted, Catholics are required to always have "implicit faith" in whatever is presented by duly constituted Church authority: "To induce speculative minds to think disparagingly of the infallibility of the Church, and to conceive that... either the teaching church or the taught church may fail," he said, will lead people to place "the disciple above the Master" or to place "private judgment above the doctrinal authority of the Church."[11]

Newman replied that this and a stream of similar retorts merely illustrated "the poor health and malfunction" of the Church in his own day. The "fullness of the whole body" absolutely required that *conspiratio* — that cooperation — of clergy and laity, and he did not see it happening in England, as was well illustrated by the hierarchy's unilateral decision to spurn the school commission. The laity must consent to be educated on their proper role in the Church, he argued, so that intellectual and spiritual growth could occur "at the same time and in the same place." The clergy, on the other hand, must cease their spiritual apartheid and begin to trust their people — for example, by establishing at various universities "a middle station where clergy and laity can meet, so as to learn to understand and to yield to each other."[12]

Bishop Ullathorne insisted that Newman had used "consult" in too sweeping a way, but then strove during the years ahead to use his office to resolve the issue. Msgr. Henry Edward Manning, vicar general (later cardinal-archbishop) of Westminster and a chronic thorn in Newman's side, was less acerbic than usual in this instance; he suggested that a follow-up treatise on "the office of the Holy Ghost" might help clear the confusion in the minds of common readers.

In September, criticism of *Consulting the Faithful* took a more ominous tone. Gillow and Bishop George Brown of Newport wrote to Archbishop Bedini, secretary of the Congregation of Propaganda in Rome, airing their concern that the effect that Newman and other Anglican converts were having "on original Catholics" could only foster Protestant notions. Gillow said, "It is most painful to see published by one whom we regarded as the best of our converts allegations and arguments...which might now seem to be the writing of a Calvinist."[13] Brown called Newman's comments about a temporary "suspense" of the Church's teaching authority "sophisticated and dishonest." "Perhaps," he said, "the high authority of the Holy See is the best to deal with the case."

Gillow, whose ire continued to mount, called the *Rambler* article "the most alarming Phenomenon of our times and [it] has made the old Catholics feel that they do not know where they can place their confidence." Newman and his associates "have a strong party," he said. "They have got into their hands the chief portion of the Catholic press, and if the breach continues to open as it is now doing, we shall see sad results."[14]

Since the storm showed no signs of dissipating, the Congregation of Propaganda took up the case formally toward the end of 1859. Bishop Ullathorne was informed that Pope Pius himself was *beaucoup peine* (much pained) by developments in England.

In January, Newman urged Cardinal Wiseman, archbishop of Westminster, who was in Rome at the time, to obtain a list of the offensive statements from his article, so that he could prepare a response. It appears that Wiseman did get such a list but neglected to pass it on to Newman — at least for several years. In June 1861, eighteen months after the article's publication, officials in Rome asked Ullathorne why Newman had not yet responded.

Newman was deeply distressed, very near depression, and could hardly have been blamed if he believed that a more sinister *conspiratio* had been hatched in his regard. Though he remained active on several intellectual and educational fronts, his literary output was greatly diminished. "I thought I had got into a scrape," he later wrote, "and it became me to be silent. So they thought at Rome."[15]

Meanwhile, his theory about the laity continued to inspire outrage in many quarters. "It is perfectly true that a cloud has been hanging over Dr. Newman" since the *Rambler* article, a prominent ecclesiastic, Msgr. George Talbot, wrote to Wiseman, "and none of his writings have removed that cloud." If ordinary Catholics take Newman's message to heart, he warned, "they will be the rulers of the Catholic Church in England instead of the Holy See and the Episcopate." Talbot then penned a few last lines, which, more than anything else, reflected the chasm between clergy and laity of his day: "What is the province of the laity? To hunt, to shoot, to entertain. These matters they understand, but to meddle with ecclesiastical matters they have no right at all, and this affair of Newman is a matter purely ecclesiastical. . . . Dr. Newman is the most dangerous man in England, and you will see that he will make use of the laity against your Grace."[16]

It is not clear exactly when Newman learned the precise nature of the charges in Rome, but he certainly had them in hand in 1867, eight years after the *Rambler* article. At that point his case in Rome was still moving forward and had been put into theological form by Cardinal John Baptist Franzelin, a close advisor of the pope, presumably for some kind of disciplinary decision. However, Newman was soon informed that efforts by Ullathorne and others to remove the threat had succeeded. It was recommended that he simply take notice of the objections and clarify his position while writing "on some related matter," and the whole controversy would be allowed to pass. This Newman did in 1871 when he produced a new edition of his book *The Arians of the Fourth Century.* None of his alterations affected the argument and claims of "Consulting the Faithful." Nor did they persuade Gillow, Talbot, and others that he was a less dangerous threat.

In the years that remained Newman strove to raise the level of thinking among the Catholic laity, though his most ambitious project, a Catholic center at Oxford University, was blocked. Two of his best known works were published: *A Grammar of Assent* and *Apologia Pro Vita Sua.* Yet, he did not easily recover from the paralyzing experience he had undergone. Indeed, during the fifteen years between 1859 and 1874, Newman, long accustomed to producing a book a year, wrote only three, and he indicated some years after the crisis that a cloud still hovered overhead:

> This age of the Church is peculiar. In former times, primitive or medieval, there was not the extreme centralization which now is in use. If a private theologian said anything free, another answered him. If the controversy grew, then it went to a Bishop, a theological faculty, or to some foreign University. The Holy See was but the court of ultimate appeal. Now, if I, as a private priest, put anything into print, Propaganda answers me at once. How can I fight with such a chain on my arm?[17]

In 1878 Pope Pius IX died and his successor, Leo XIII, removed the chain by making the seventy-eight-year-old Newman a cardinal the following year. Newman was euphoric. "The cloud is lifted from me forever," he said.[18] He lived on for another eleven years, enjoying his vindication. But he was never to see the full extent of his legacy.

NEWMAN'S FOOTPRINTS

Theologians, educators, and historians were mining the insights of John Henry Newman long before he died, and new examinations of his work are still being produced. His influence on modern interpretations of the Church and Church authority are profound. It would be an exaggeration to assert that the teaching Church today fully endorses the concepts of "sense of the faithful" and *conspiratio* that so engaged his mind and heart.

Yet, Newman's insistence that doctrine is not handed down from above in final form but "develops" over time is now accepted (sometimes begrudgingly) at every level of Church authority. In addition, Newman's assertion that "consultation" is essential in the formation of doctrine is endorsed by theologians as a given. For example, in a discussion of the pope's authority in the book *Magisterium,* Jesuit theologian Francis Sullivan says, "Before the pope can define a dogma, he must listen to the Church, and he can define...only what he finds in the faith of the Church. The pope has no source of revelation that is independent of the faith-life of the Church....The pope simply cannot define a dogma of faith without having in some real way consulted the faith of the Church."[19] Sullivan taught for some thirty years at the Gregorian University in Rome, where scores of current American bishops were educated. And his book *Magisterium* has been long considered an authoritative text in seminary education. Finally, Newman's once controversial and "dangerous" emphasis on the laity's full participation as a requirement if the Church is to achieve its "fullness" has been virtually canonized. His fingerprints are all over the documents of Vatican II.

They show up especially in the Dogmatic Constitution on the Church, which presents infallibility not as a monopoly of the teaching church but a shared gift of the Holy Spirit:

> The body of the faithful as a whole, anointed by the Holy One, cannot err in matters of belief....Allotting His gifts "to everyone according as He will...," [the Holy Spirit] distributes special graces among the faithful of every rank....He makes them fit and ready to undertake the various tasks and offices for the upbuilding and renewal of the Church....Christ, the great Prophet who proclaimed the Kingdom of God, continually fulfills His prophetic office...not only through the hierarchy who teach in His name...but also through the laity. For that very purpose He made them His witnesses and gave them understanding of the faith and the gift of speech.[20]

The Newman fingerprints show up too in the Decree on the Apostolate of the Laity, which insists that the "priestly, prophetic and royal office of Christ" is shared by all lay members of the Church. "They are consecrated into a royal priesthood and a holy people.... The 'passive' apostolate of merely leading the 'good life' is not sufficient for the Christian today. They must 'preach' the gospel to Christian and non-Christian alike."[21]

Newman's influence can be found as well in the council documents on revelation, priestly formation, ecumenism, and education. In his book *Newman and the Modern World*, Christopher Hollis attributes the outgoing, optimistic, inclusive approach that was so characteristic of Vatican II and of Pope John XXIII to Newman's influence. "There is an almost total contrast between the language of the Vatican of a hundred years ago [Vatican I] and that of Pope John," he wrote, "and the major fact in Catholic history that stands between those days and this — the major cause of the change of language — has been the writing of Newman."[22]

Pope Paul VI in 1963 paid special tribute to Newman, speaking of him as "the promoter and representative of the Oxford movement, which raised so many religious questions and excited such great spiritual energies ... who in full consciousness of his mission ... and guided solely by love of the truth and fidelity to Christ, traced an itinerary the most toilsome but also the greatest, the most meaningful, the most conclusive that human thought ever traveled during the last century, indeed one might say during the modern era, to arrive at the fullness of wisdom and grace."

Vatican II, he said, was "Newman's council."[23]

FOUR

MARY WARD
No Ordinary Woman

At the age of twenty-four, Mary Ward faced a major crisis of faith. She had already been trying for four years to determine what God wanted her to do, so she scrupulously followed the recommendations of her spiritual directors and advisors. Yet she was always restless, always torn by a conflict between their advice and a mysterious "some other thing" to which she felt called. The problem was not her vocation to religious life. From the age of fifteen, she knew she was meant to be a religious sister, she was meant to serve. The question was what kind of sister, what kind of service.

Mary Ward had traveled from her native England to St. Omer in the Spanish Netherlands in 1605. Roman Catholics in England were undergoing persecution at the time, and religious orders were strictly banned. St. Omer, which boasted a large, Jesuit-run seminary and growing communities of Benedictine, Augustinian, and Franciscan sisters, had become a gathering place for Catholic refugees. On arrival, Ward thought she might enter one of these larger orders as a novice, but her first contact, a Jesuit professor of morality, assured her that her real vocation was to the cloistered Flemish Poor Clare sisters, who just happened at that time to need a lay sister to carry out an array of duties in and around the convent. Ward consented and stayed with the Poor Clares for more than a year. It was a period she later described as "full of aversion and grief." She was guided, she said, "entirely by way of fear, for instance that I ought to hate myself, to fear the judgment of God, to tremble at the pains of hell, in all of which I was most inept. To labor through love, even death appeared to me to be easy, but fear made...little impression."[1] In 1607, while praying about the troubled situation in her homeland, she was deeply moved to reach out to English Catholics in some tangible way. She convinced her spiritual advisor that she should help organize a new foundation of English Poor Clares in the Netherlands, and permission was granted. During her first month in this new endeavor, Mary Ward made a retreat using the Spiritual Exercises of St. Ignatius. It was directed by Fr. Roger Lee, who became her spiritual director for many years.

Within a few months, she was restless again and informed Lee that this place was not for her either. He counseled her to calm down and suggested that perhaps her real calling was to the highly ascetic, more strictly cloistered, Carmelite order. To relieve herself of constant anxiety, Ward made a vow to God to join the Carmelites if Lee commanded that. The distress only mounted. She was beginning to think her real calling was to found an entirely new religious order of women — one combining an interior life of prayer and contemplation and an exterior life of preaching the gospel and doing good works in the world, just as the Jesuits were doing. Why, she wondered, should not women as well as men respond to the pressing needs of the time? Yet she remained "fearful of believing... [something] to be good which was not so."

Thus her crisis: to follow the time-honored practice of giving unquestioning obedience to the wise counselors and confessors, the "ghostly fathers" who stood in God's place, or to follow the dim, unpaved road that God seemed to be stretching out before her. "To resist that which now operated in me I could not," she later wrote, "and to have a will in opposition to the vow, I ought not. In this conflict, giving myself to prayer, I protested to God...that I had not and would not admit on this occasion any other will than his."

After several more months, she was fully convinced that continuing in her present situation would be intolerable. It was love, she said, that was impelling her. "In these two contraries," she said, "God could not be against himself."[2] She returned to England.

There Ward experienced an unexpected sense of calm that remained with her, even though much of her career would involve a struggle to balance the obligations of authority against the insistent inspiration that flowed out of her spiritual life.

In England she taught religion among the poor and visited prisons. Gradually she worked out the essentials of her new religious order, sharing her enthusiasm and plans with a small group of other young women. Unlike the communities of sisters she experienced on the Continent, this one would be totally unenclosed and uncloistered, with the members having no restrictions on movement; they would live in the world, in the areas where they worked; they would wear the conventional, secular dress of the time; the entire operation would be organized and governed solely by the women themselves; they would follow, insofar as practical, "the matter and manner" of the Society of Jesus; and they would be answerable only to God and the pope.

In 1610 Ward and six like-minded women returned to St. Omer and opened a school for the daughters of English refugees. She clarified in her own mind and on paper the details of this "mode of life," which would come to be known as the Institute of the Blessed Virgin Mary (IBVM):

> We propose to follow a mixed kind of life, such a life as we hold Christ our Lord and Master to have taught his disciples; such a life as his Blessed Mother seems to have led...and many holy virgins and widows;...that we more easily instruct virgins and young girls from their earliest years in piety, Christian morals and the liberal arts that they may afterwards, according to their respective vocations, profitably embrace either the secular or the religious state.[3]

"NO AUTHORITY OF THEIR OWN"

Mary Ward was well aware that her new creation was flying in the face of explicit directives from the Council of Trent, which concluded twenty-two years before her birth. In the no-nonsense regimentation that marked the Counter-Reformation era, the council ordered all bishops "under the judgement of God and pain of eternal malediction" to ensure that all nuns under their jurisdictions live in total enclosure. After her formal profession, said Trent, "it shall be unlawful for any nun to go out of her convent, even for a short period, under any pretext whatever, except for some lawful cause which must be explicitly approved by the bishop."[4] Their religious perfection was to be sought in total separation from the outer world. If certain convents resisted regulations of cloister, local bishops were authorized to seek the assistance of civil authorities in forcing compliance.

To be sure, earlier in the sixteenth century, women's religious orders had been involved in apostolic activity, especially education of children and nursing. One of the most successful of these was the Ursuline Order, founded in Italy by the tireless and resourceful Angela Merici. The members cared for orphans, rehabilitated prostitutes, helped laborers recover their due wages, settled disputes among property owners, raised the funds needed for their work, and in other ways operated as an all-purpose religious and social agency. The Ursulines were regarded in some quarters as a women's incarnation of the Jesuits. But the Council of Trent was determined to rein in largely independent organizations of this kind. According to Jo Ann McNamara, a historian of religious women,

> The real issue was not cloistering but clerical control. Restriction on religious women previously left free for charitable work fitted into a larger pattern of restriction on private social enterprise. Protestant countries abolished confraternities and Catholic monarchs circumscribed them as disruptive of the social order. The Council of Trent subjected [all] charitable organizations to episcopal visitation and gave bishops control over pious legacies.[5]

These restrictions were imposed more rigorously on women's groups because of the prevailing societal and religious attitudes toward women in general. In his study of canonical regulations regarding enclosure, James Cain said that the juridical status of woman in that period was "one of complete subjection to the dominion of man, having no authority of her own."[6] A contemporary spiritual directory suggested that when the Ignatian Exercises were taken by women, "the same method should be followed...as [is followed] with persons of little education, unless one or other among the women should have the capacity for spiritual things."[7]

As her upstart institute attracted new members to St. Omer, Ward did not overtly question the common assumptions about women and never disputed the legislation of the council. Operating out of a grounded sense of confidence in her mission, she simply acted as if neither existed.

A "RECUSANT" CHILDHOOD

That stance can be better understood in light of Mary Ward's experience as a girl growing up in Yorkshire, England, long before her first trip to the Continent. Though the Church of England became the state-supported, official faith under King Henry VIII, a quiet, widespread resistance lingered in parts of the country. After Queen Elizabeth was excommunicated by a papal bull in 1570, the English monarch took punitive steps against these "recusants" (those who clung to the Roman Catholic faith). Among them were Mary Ward's parents, Marmaduke and Ursula, and large numbers of their relatives and associates. Yorkshire, in fact, came to be regarded as a hotbed of recusant resistance. Fines or imprisonment were exacted against any who failed to show up for Anglican services, and Catholic priests were hunted down and imprisoned or executed.

Evidence of the Ward family's non-cooperation is plentiful in the old records. Ursula's first husband was jailed for resistance in 1580 and died in prison two years later. Urusla herself was required to pay substantial fines, and the household was in a continuous state of upheaval throughout Mary's early life due to pressure on the family by the authorities. From the ages of five to ten, she spent much of her time with her grandmother, Ursula Wright, who had survived fourteen years in prison and was still listed in town records as "a popishe recusant." As a teenager, Mary lived for periods with other Yorkshire families notorious for their resistance. At least three relatives were executed for allegedly conspiring in the Gunpowder Plot in 1605, the year she first went to St. Omer.[8]

Mary Ward was therefore acutely aware of the problems confronting the old faith and the need for education and support for the recusants; a closed, monastic life did not seem to her an adequate response to the special signs of the times.

She had also observed in her youth a peculiar characteristic of Catholic resistance in England. Husbands often attended Anglican services, required seventy or more times a year in order to avoid penalties, while their wives would not conform in any way and were accordingly subject to fines and imprisonment. In some cases, the husbands resented their wives' stubbornness. In other cases, Church of England authorities suspected that those cooperating husbands were actually "dissembling schismatics and secret favorites of their wives' religion." Women's resistance became so common in the late 1500s that a law was passed allowing the state to confiscate two-thirds of a non-cooperating widow's assets, leaving her virtually penniless. The Catholic resistance in England was essentially a women's movement, according to historian John Bossy. "On few points in the early history of English Catholicism," he wrote, "is there such a unanimous convergence of evidence as on the importance of the part played by women."

Thus Ward acquired during her formative years a powerful memory of strong women, and that influence unquestionably countered for her the limited societal expectations of women in her time. The institute, she insisted, would not be subject to the control of local bishops; it would be subject to its own leadership, though the goal was to work cooperatively with the clergy of every rank as well as laity in the apostolate.

"WOMEN WILL DO MUCH"

Ward did not overstress all these IBVM innovations in the formal petition for approval that she presented to Pope Paul V in 1615. By then, the teaching work at St. Omer was going well, the contingent of women dedicated to this noncanonical religious order was growing, and calls were coming from elsewhere in Europe for assistance from the institute. Lee and other Jesuits proved helpful in these years of growth, but signs of resistance also appeared. Some Jesuits regarded the women as uppity and clearly disruptive of proper Church procedures, while opponents of the Jesuits saw the institute as exhibit number one of Jesuit-inspired radicalism and excess. One writer at the time acknowledged Mary Ward as "no ordinary woman," one who "possessed more than woman's share of courage and perseverance." He added, however, that she and her companions were under the spell of "crafty" Jesuits who knew how to establish an "intimate relationship" with these helpless women, transforming them into "female Jesuits," and using them "for carrying out their policies."[9]

Meanwhile, the pope gave the IBVM petition an ambiguous and cautious temporary approval, noting that full, formal recognition would depend on an examination of the order by the appropriate Vatican congregations. Ward was delighted and established new foundations in the next few years in Liege, Belgium; Cologne and Trier, Germany; and at London and Suffolk, England. Ward herself spearheaded the English effort. Here her members could move about somewhat freely, since they wore no distinctive, religious garb. Despite the precautions they took, several institute members were arrested and imprisoned for a time. According to one report, Ward was apprehended in London in 1618, and "a sentence of death was passed upon her for religion, but there was no execution for fear of odium." The "fear of odium" apparently referred to a concern by English authorities that her death might trigger a violent uprising by the recusants.

On her return to St. Omer, Ward praised her companions for what they were achieving: "There was a Father that lately came into England whom I heard say that he would not for a thousand of worlds be a woman, because he thought a woman could not apprehend God. I answered nothing, but only smiled, although I could have answered him by the experience I have of the contrary. I could have been sorry for his want...not want of judgment, for he is a man of very good judgment; his want is in experience."[10] She foresaw a different kind of attitude toward women in the Church and was anxious for its appearance. "I hope in God it will be seen in time that women in time will do much," she said.

By the early 1620s storm clouds were converging. Some Jesuits mocked these "galloping girls" of unlimited energy who seemed to be everywhere; other critics saw them as a real threat to the clerical status quo. Important members of the English clergy, who had a representative in Rome, began lobbying for suppression of the institute. "They cited the boldness of women who seek to instruct others in the catechism and bring them to acts of contrition and meditation, whose lives resemble those of the laity, and who cause great scandal by their lack of enclosure." A truly severe blow struck when the Jesuit general, Mutius Vitelleschi, in 1622 prohibited any member of the society from providing further assistance, advice, or encouragement to the IBVMs. It had been through the good offices of the Jesuits that Ward had been able to break through the red tape and suspicion in many cities where she sought to set up schools and foundations. Vitelleschi's remarks suggested that he had not taken this step on his own but had been ordered from above.

Ever resilient, Ward took the initiative. Nine years had passed in silence since she sought official Church approbation, so she petitioned again, this time in 1624, to the new pope, Urban VIII. His reaction was less than encouraging: he immediately ordered the closing of the IBVM foundations in Rome and elsewhere in Italy, but said and did nothing more. Ward, it seems, chose to take the rebuke as a mysterious gesture of approval, so she opened new houses soon after in Munich, Vienna, and Pressburg. In her writings she referred often to Loyola's emphasis on detachment and resignation, urging her associates to keep themselves "in balance," since everything depends on God's "liberality," of which all of them had already received a "more than full measure."[11] She reminded them too that as Christians they stood under the banner of the cross and must be prepared to endure "the long loneliness" — the deprivation of human support and sometimes even of the sense of God's presence.[12]

In early 1628 the Congregation of Propaganda established a special commission to investigate these English sisters. Completing its deliberations with unaccustomed swiftness, the committee recommended that the "Jesuitesses" be suppressed. In his report, the secretary of the congregation, Msgr. Francesco Ingoli, called the institute the fruit of an ill-advised collaboration between a Jesuit of limited education (Roger Lee) and a "former Poor Clare nun of a masculine cast of mind." He labeled Ward's companions "proud, with a mania for liberty and garrulous." Ward's contention that the extreme needs of the time should excuse institute members from the requirement of enclosure he dismissed as irrelevant. The Church's statutes hold first priority, he said, and it "matters little" what the times require.

A year passed and still there was no absolute directive from the Vatican. Ward obtained an audience with Pope Urban and argued her case: the IBVM educational initiatives were flourishing in a dozen cities; the community was growing in numbers; and its critics misunderstood or exaggerated her activities and intentions. Urban listened but still said nothing definitive.

So another year went by. Many members of the institute, besieged by rumors and continuing criticism (much of it from the clergy), became agitated and wondered if they should begin closing down operations. Ward, as usual, counseled patience.

In late 1630 she again petitioned the pope for approval of the institute:

> It is now ... twenty-five years since I left my native country and parents.... Ten years I employed in prayer, fasting and penance, and other things suitable for such a result, to learn [in] what order of religion or mode of life I was to spend my days. That which unworthily I now profess, and by the mercy of God for twenty-two years practised, was totally and entirely, as far as human judgement can arrive, ordained and commended to me by the express word of Him who will not deceive, nor can be deceived.[13]

She would disband the order if so ordered, she said, but she would under no circumstances alter the basic structure, because she remained convinced that its form had been "ordained and commanded by God."

"HERETIC, SCHISMATIC, REBEL"

At last the long-awaited decision came — and it was devastating. In the papal bull *Pastoralis romani pontifici,* published in January of 1631, five weeks after Ward's latest petition, Urban suppressed the institute and any other noncanonical groups like it, all of which he referred to as "pernicious growths":

> We have learned, not without great displeasure, that in several parts of Italy and beyond the mountains, certain women or vir-

gins take the name of Jesuitesses without an approbation from the Holy See. Being gathered for several years under the pretext of living the religious life, they have . . . founded buildings in the form of colleges; they have erected houses of probation. They have a superior general over their pretended congregation and have made vows in her hands . . . in imitation of the solemn vows; they go freely everywhere without respect for the laws of cloister under the pretext of working for the salvation of souls; and they are accustomed to undertake . . . other works very little in conformity with the weakness of their sex and their spirit . . . [and little in conformity] with feminine modesty and above all with virginal shame . . . works many highly distinguished in the science of sacred letters would only undertake with difficulty and with great circumspection.[14]

The IBVM members were informed that their vows were dissolved, that they could admit no more recruits, and that they must shut down all their schools and foundations. They were given the alternatives of joining an established religious order, finding local bishops under whose regulations they could work, or entering the honorable state of matrimony.

In Munich at the time, Mary Ward soon heard the news, but she was ill and took no immediate action until she could see a published copy of the bull. The Vatican would countenance no delays. In February, Ward was formally accused by the Office of the Inquisition of being a "heretic, schismatic and rebel to the Holy Church." She was arrested by civil authorities and put in a Munich prison without being given any idea when, if ever, she would be released. Fearing she would die there, she asked for the sacraments and was told that all such consolations were denied until such times as she renounced her heresy. She regarded a retraction as "betrayal of the many innocent and deserving persons who supported me," and said she would therefore forgo the sacraments, relying entirely on the mercy of God.

To Urban she wrote, "I have never done or said anything either great or small against his Holiness . . . or the authority of Holy Church. But on the contrary, my feeble powers and labours have been for twenty-six years entirely . . . employed for the honour and service of both, as I hope, by the mercy of God and the benignity of His Holiness, will be manifested in due time and place."[15]

She also wrote to the distressed members of the institute, urging them to be "expedite and quietly industrious . . . in the business" and to commend the case to God "that He would vouchsafe to enlighten and forgive all and would use all you do to his honour. . . . Let us let God do what He will in His turn."[16] (Her letters from prison were written in lemon juice, apparently to make them illegible to her jailers.) Ward's stay in prison lasted two months. Upon her release she tried to assist members of the now dissolved institute establish new lives, and she never spoke a word against the pope or her other critics and enemies.

Two years after publication of the bull, Urban relented a bit, withdrawing the personal charges of heresy and schism against Ward and allowing former institute members to continue living in Rome if they wished to do so. He emphasized, however, that he was not rescinding any of the other provisions of the bull.

Officially, the Institute of the Blessed Virgin Mary simply went out of existence for a time, and there is no way to measure the extent of that loss. The impact was perhaps greatest in England where the IBVMs had operated clandestinely among the Catholic recusants for twenty years. Said historian John Bossy, "If I were asked to choose a single incident to illustrate the turn of the tide [against Roman Catholicism in England], I would suggest the rejection of the ideal and practice embodied in Mary Ward's Institute of Mary." In rejecting it, he said, Church officials put the law over the spirit, abandoned the Catholic cause, and thereby "missed the boat for a couple of generations."[17]

THE ORDER RESURRECTED

Ward returned to England, and for her remaining fourteen years lived as a layperson with a group of close companions, teaching and catechizing when possible. In a letter to veterans of the IBVM struggle in 1645, the year of her death, she asked them to always see "the practice of God's vocation" in whatever they did and to love freely without expecting recognition or reward. Nor should they grieve over her. "It matters not the who but the what," she said. "And when God will enable me to be in place I will serve you."[18]

As it turned out, several former IBVM members, later joined by other women, took her words to heart and continued to live as quasi-religious in several areas, maintaining the basics of the institute, including freedom from enclosure. In 1703, some seventy-two years after the fateful bull, the successors of this group won approval from Pope Clement XI. Then, in 1877, Pope Pius IX gave final and official approbation to the order, which was growing rapidly. By the early twentieth century it had schools and foundations on every continent, and it continues to this day. Yet, it was only in 1909, 224 years after Ward's birth, that the modern IBVMs were allowed to identify her as their foundress. Her gradual rehabilitation reached a peak in 1951. At the World Congress of the Lay Apostolate in Rome, Pope Pius XII called Mary Ward "that incomparable woman given by Catholic England to the Church in the darkest and most blood-stained of periods."[19]

Her insights gained a measure of recognition in Vatican II's Decree on the Appropriate Renewal of the Religious Life. As the essential starting of renewal, said the council, two simultaneous processes must occur: first, "a continuous return to the sources of all Christian life," and second, "an adjustment of the community to the changed conditions of the times." In addition, noted the bishops,

> It serves the best interests of the Church for communities to have their own special character and purpose.... Communities should promote among their members a suitable awareness of contemporary human conditions and of the needs of the Church. For if their members can combine the burning zeal of an apostle with wise judgments made in the light of faith concerning the circumstances of the modern world, they will be able to come to the aid of men more effectively.[20]

Today, the vital ingredients of most Catholic religious orders are these: the blending of contemplation and action, freedom from enclosure, the optional wearing of contemporary dress, the managing of their own affairs, and an eagerness to adjust in response to the challenges of the age. And accordingly, Mary Ward must be regarded as a pioneer whose vision surpassed the limitations of the time in which she lived.

In her book *Love — the Driving Force: Mary Ward's Spirituality*, Jeanne Cover, herself an IBVM sister, marvels at the almost preternatural equanimity Ward displayed through her long saga. Cover finds an explanation in what Ward described in her writings as the "estate of justice": It was an orientation of mind and soul that she developed following her early, restless activities with the Poor Clares, and it provided her with a unique sense of freedom. In her estate of justice Ward found a way to harmonize the seemingly irreconcilable conflict between obedience to the law and the movement of the Spirit within her. She loved the Church in its fullness — and that meant doing what needed to be done even if it required the bypassing of certain institutional restrictions and then letting "God do what He will in His turn."[21]

FIVE

THE JESUITS AND USURY
A Doctrine Not Received

The most intriguing thing about the great usury conflict in the sixteenth century is that no one said, "Look, the whole economic system has been permanently altered, the meaning of money has changed, the old guidelines are outmoded!" And no one said, "Stop your quibbling and looking for loopholes and piling distinctions on top of one another; the bottom line is the same as it always was: Thou shalt not steal."

No one said these things, because the world was caught in a historical vortex, and it appeared to many that society was plunging headlong into catastrophe. The reigning moral authorities, some of them the smartest and holiest people of their day, felt obliged to condemn the borrowing and lending of money at interest, as their predecessors had always done in the past. Yet, they could neither stop nor understand the momentum — they were too close to the problem. From our vantage point, some four hundred years later, we can sympathize with their concern. We can also observe how the problem was finally resolved through the providential interplay of various forces, not the least of which was public dissent.

In the year 1565, when Charles Borromeo became the bishop of Milan, he found himself in a Middle Age metropolis, a center of intense cultural and economic activity. Citizens elsewhere might be concerned with the continuing fallout from the Protestant Reformation, but in Milan the operative word was "business": continuous buying and selling and trading and importing and exporting and opening of shops and expansion of already existing enterprises — almost all of it made possible by the extension of credit and the borrowing and lending of money at interest. For Charles Borromeo, a zealous defender of the faith and a man well on his way to sainthood, the operative word here was "usury." Were these good people unaware, he wondered, that the lending of money at interest was sinful? Did they not know that the Scriptures, the Fathers, the popes, and the great councils had spoken against this practice for fifteen hundred years with a single, uncontradicted voice? Were they unaware that they were trafficking in something intrinsically evil and mortally sinful?

Borromeo, of course, understood what was occurring and why. In the old feudal system, which had prevailed in Christendom for centuries, the great estates were ruled over by local lords and their descendants. The masses who lived in and around these closed, self-contained agricultural settlements were bound together by clearly defined sets of mutual rights and obligations. Everything worked smoothly as long as people knew and accepted their place. Borrowing and lending were unnecessary except during periods of famine. Money was an inert, seldom used medium of exchange. The Church's clear doctrine on interest had always been taught, lest anyone be tempted to step out of line and try to make a profit on somebody else's misery.

But the old feudal system had been gradually coming apart over a period of several centuries. Trading routes were now opened to the East; food was being produced not just for local consumption but also for export; new inventions led to new industries and businesses; banks were springing up everywhere, no longer serving only the privileged but also those common folk who were eager to seize opportunity and raise their meager standard of living.

All this Charles Borromeo knew, and he could only regard it as a culture of greed, something detestable in the eyes of God. So he called a synod of his priests and led them on an excursion through Church history and theology. No fewer than twelve popes and three ecumenical councils, he explained, had flatly condemned the taking of any interest on a loan and pronounced the strongest penalties against anyone who engaged in such activity.

"LEND HOPING NOTHING THEREBY"

The Second Lateran Council, in the twelfth century, was typically explicit:

> We condemn that detestable, shameful, and insatiable rapacity of money lenders, which has been denounced by divine and human laws and throughout the Old and New Testaments, and we deprive them of all ecclesiastical consolation, commanding that no archbishop, no abbot of any order, nor anyone in clerical orders shall, except with the utmost caution, dare to receive usurers; but throughout their life let them be stigmatized with the mark of infamy, and unless they repent let them be deprived of Christian burial.[1]

Pope Clement V was no less direct almost two hundred years later:

> If anyone falls into the error of believing and affirming that it is not a sin to practice usury, we decree that he be punished as a heretic, and we strictly command the ordinaries...and the inquisitors to proceed against those suspected of such errors in the same way as they would proceed against those accused publicly or suspected of heresy.[2]

The *Roman Catechism,* of which Bishop Borromeo was a principal author, nicely summed up the Church's rationale:

> Whatever is received beyond the principal,...whether it be money or whether it be any other thing which can be purchased or estimated in money, is usury; for it is written in Ezekiel, "He has not lent at usury nor received an increase," and in Luke the Lord says, "Lend hoping nothing thereby." This was always a most grave crime, even among the gentiles, and especially odious. Hence the question, "What is usury?" is answered, "What is it to kill a man?" Those who commit usury sell the same thing twice or sell what is not.[3]

Borromeo reminded the faithful that nothing beyond the return of the principal may be required in a loan transaction, and he ordered his priests to enforce the divine law — to deny absolution to anyone practicing usury. But he knew that enforcement would not be easy, because four distinct kinds of interest taking had become inveterate in his diocese. And some theologians, contrary to Church teaching, were telling the people that they could accept these practices in good conscience.

• The first, called the "triple contract," looked upon a loan as a kind of partnership between the lender and borrower, and was popular whenever the lender faced a substantial risk of losing the investment. In this situation the lender would take out insurance guaranteeing that his principal would be repaid. He might also take out insurance guaranteeing that he would make a small profit on the loan. The lender would expect to be reimbursed for these insurance premiums when the principal was returned.

• The second concerned several new forms of annuity that operated much like interest-paying loans. In their old form, annuities were common and no cause for concern. If, for example, a person gave a farmer a lump sum with the expectation of a yearly payment depending on the farm's yield for that year, moral theologians had no problem. The newer annuities expected, among other things, a set return on the lump sum regardless of whether the farmer had a good or bad year.

• The third involved the buying and selling of foreign currency, a practice that had grown as business operators traveled more frequently across national borders. The exchange of money was considered morally justified, but a new practice, much encouraged by exchange bankers, allowed for the purchase of foreign currency with delivery scheduled for a later date; the profit that the seller of the currency made in this situation seemed very much like the profit on a loan.

• Fourth, people were beginning to deposit their surplus funds in banks, which needed large sums of money on hand for business loans and were happy to mete out a modicum of interest even for small deposits.

The majority of Catholic theologians regarded all these newer manifestations as sinful. But an articulate minority, mostly from the

University of Tübingen, argued publicly and insistently that these were all exceptions to the general ban on interest taking. And the citizens of Milan in overwhelming numbers accepted this minority position.

Borromeo's hopes that his priests would restore compliance with the old morality proved to be in vain. Two years after the synod, nothing had changed except an increase in contracts involving interest. Bishop Borromeo besought the pope to take a stand. Perhaps, he thought, an updated papal condemnation would awaken Christians.

"DIFFICULTIES" TO BE OVERCOME

Meanwhile, in Augsburg, Bavaria, another banking capital, a similar scenario was playing itself out. The Jesuit Peter Canisius found evidence of all the above-mentioned forms of lending, plus a more overt practice: people were lending money at a flat 5 percent without even bothering to determine how this might be construed an exception to the usury law. Real usury, he told the Augsburg clergy, "is here openly committed and the divine commandment 'Lend freely hoping nothing thereby' is violated."[4] The zealous Canisius, who, like Borromeo, would attain formal sanctity soon after his death, ordered all Jesuits under his supervision to deny absolution to anyone taking part in a 5 percent loan. But the secular priests of Augsburg, accustomed to this so-called German loan, refused to go along. As a result, 5 percent loaners could get absolution in the secular churches of Augsburg but not in the Jesuit churches. Frustrated, Canisius too sought a firm statement from the pope.

Over in Liechtenstein, Ursula Fugger, a member by marriage of the prominent and wealthy Fugger banking family and herself a recent convert to the Catholic faith, appealed for assistance to the Jesuit general in Rome, Francis Borgia. "What are we to do," she wrote, "about the usurious contracts in which our family is not a little entangled?"[5] Her concern was not only for the eternal destiny of her husband and in-laws, but also for the temporal prosperity of her own children, since profit made from usury could not be lawfully passed on as an inheritance to the next generation in Catholic regions. Borgia, another early Jesuit saint, sympathized with Ursula's worry and assured her that a commission was already preparing a recommendation for the pope.

The commission, in fact, had just been appointed as a result of the pleas of Borromeo, Canisius, and Borgia.

It was not, however, until 1569, two years after Canisius sought papal aid, that the pope, Pius V (he too a man destined for canonization), issued the bull *Cum onus*. It dealt mainly with annuities and basically condemned all the new forms of such contracts as "a grave disease and deadly poison." In addition, he ruled as intrinsically evil the 5 percent contracts so popular in Germany. Anyone attempting to contradict his authority in this matter, said Pius, should be aware that "he has incurred the wrath of almighty God and his blessed apostles Peter and Paul."[6]

As far as Canisius was concerned, at least two manifestations of the evil were thus scuttled. He wrote to the pope, "I know that for certain one's execution of this recent judgment will be displeasing and harsh...but with Christ as our leader we shall overcome these difficulties on the part of those hearing confessions and on the part of those confessing."[7]

But then Pius himself upset this new status quo by stating soon after that "miserable" people — that is, widows, wards of the state, and disabled persons who entered into 5 percent contracts — might be "excused." How, asked the baffled moralists, could something intrinsically evil ever be excusable?

As a result, the Jesuits formed their own, unofficial commission to sort through the difficulties and seeming contradictions. The group was headed by Francisco Toledo — a highly regarded advisor to the Vatican — several Jesuit provincials, and a variety of moral theologians. The commission did something that previous bodies studying usury had never done: it heard arguments favoring acceptance of the new practices from representatives of the Fuggers and other lay persons directly involved in banking and lending. The body also consulted the eminent Spanish theologian Navarrus, who acknowledged that the experience of the laity had an influence on his moral judgments. "An infinite number of decent Christians," he said, are engaged in exchange banking or other interest-providing activities, and he objected to an analysis that would "damn the whole world."[8] Since Navarrus had drafted much of the *Cum onus* bull, he was asked how obligatory its provisions were. It appeared, he said, that some provisions were based on divine or natural law and therefore permitted no exceptions, while others were from positive, papal law and did permit exceptions. But he left the Jesuits somewhat confused about which was which.

Just about this time Pope Pius issued a second bull, *In eam.* In it he condemned in the harshest terms those forms of exchange banking involving the purchase of foreign currency with delivery expected later. He also ruled simple bank deposits a clear example of usury and absolutely forbidden. In effect, then, these two documents declared immoral almost any transaction that generated real profit.

CONTRADICTION AND CONFUSION

Only after Pius's death, in 1573, did the Jesuit commission come forth with its own recommendations. The members agreed with the pope on some matters, disagreed on others. For example, the basic 5 percent contract was immoral, they said, even for widows and other "miserable" persons. But they found the triple contract and some new forms of annuity (which were virtually the equivalent of 5 percent contracts) to be acceptable, despite the papal ruling.

This further troubled the waters. Who was right, the pope or the commission? In Augsburg, where the 5 percent contract was commonplace, Peter Canisius convinced the bishop to require his secular priests to enforce the ban on these contracts. But when the bishop died, the new Augsburg bishop allowed his priests to ignore the ban and essentially told Canisius to mind his own business. The papal nuncio in Germany agreed with Canisius, and a professor at a Jesuit university in Germany became so incensed about the "gross disobedience" to clear papal orders that he mounted a public campaign to root out 5 percent contracts. This in turn infuriated the banking and business communities, which were following the more permissive lead of the new bishop, the secular priests, and a growing number of Jesuits who disagreed with Canisius.

In an effort to calm the storm, the new pope, Gregory XIII, decreed that all Jesuits must refuse to absolve those participating in 5 percent arrangements. On the other hand, he also ruled that they must henceforth stop preaching or writing about the subject — either in support of the papal position or in opposition to it.

This strategy did not work. The dispute grew even louder and stretched out for more than seven years. In 1581 Bishop Borromeo of Milan begged the pope to do something, and Gregory concurred that the matter was nearly out of hand. He summoned an advisory commission, composed largely of Jesuits and including the Spanish theologian Gregory of Valencia. In contradiction of Pope Pius's bulls, the members recommended full acceptance of the triple contract and virtually all the new, liberal forms of annuity. In treating the 5 percent contract, they went into excruciating detail, distinguishing certain situations in which it might be morally acceptable and other situations in which it would be sinful.

John Noonan, a scholar who meticulously examined the sixteenth-century usury dispute in all its particulars, is hard-pressed to explain to a modern audience the tortured nuances of the commission's recommendations. For example,

> The 5 percent was to be considered usury, if it was sought by force of a loan alone; or if in a loan it was sought without pretext of title, or with false title, or with the deliberate exclusion of all titles, or in a contract not called a loan where no pretext existed. But if the person of the borrower was considered by the parties — that is if the borrower were a merchant or the owner of a fruitful land, or a working person, and the contract was made with him principally in consideration of his status — the 5 percent contract could be interpreted as either a triple contract or a real or personal *census* [annuity].[9]

Beneath the fog, the real impact was this: the 5 percent contract, in the judgment of the papal commission, was not intrinsically evil, as Pope Pius V had said; its morality was to be judged on circumstances.

Though this represented an important step forward, it was undoubtedly too much for the pope to fully accept at that point. He therefore fell back on the judgment of his saintly predecessor, Pius V, and declared that 5 percent arrangements "cannot be excused by any custom or human law." Yet, not to be outdone in distinctions, he continued:

But if in Germany there is some other contract in which 5 percent is received, which is celebrated in form and manner different from the aforesaid, we do not by this intend to condemn or approve it, unless it is particularly set out and considered that so what is to be judged in its regard may be decreed, as is decreed in regard to what has been proposed.[10]

When Duke William of Bavaria attempted to impose on his citizens by civil law Gregory's bewildering interpretations, he met wholesale resistance. He turned to Gregory of Valencia, a major force in the recent Jesuit commission. Gregory suggested that the duke could in good conscience abide by the more liberal recommendations of the Jesuit commissions and cease trying to impose the unimposable on his subjects.

Gradually then, over the next five years, most forms of interest taking so excoriated by the popes came to be accepted by theologians and laity alike. The furor died down and there were no reported repercussions by Church authorities against those who dared to reject or reinterpret papal teaching. It should be noted that this was due in no small way to the fact that many ecclesiastical leaders and organizations were themselves already steeped in the business of lending and borrowing.

ACCEPTED NOWHERE

There was to be only one more explosive attempt to turn the world around and restore the old order. In 1586 Pope Sixtus V issued his appropriately titled bull *Detestabilis avaritia,* in which he accused the devil of leading Christians "to immerse themselves in the whirlpool of usury, odious to God and men, condemned by the sacred canons, and contrary to Christian charity."[11] He castigated in particular all quasi-partnership agreements like the triple contract and implicitly forbade even those forms of annuity allowed earlier in the bulls of Pius V. But he was too late. The bull was accepted nowhere and had no effect.

During the next three hundred years there would be sporadic flare-ups of the old controversy. As late as 1821 the Holy Office of the Vatican stated that usury is against the natural law and "wrong in its essence."[12]

But by then the very meaning of the word had shifted from the taking of any interest on a loan or business deal to the taking of *excessive* or *unjust* interest. Economists by then had fully explained how money in the postmedieval world is a fertile commodity, that in good times it multiplies and grows, and that the owner of that money is entitled to the profit that comes from that growth. The ever present danger is not in profit itself but in the exploitation of another for the sake of profit.

In 1850 Pope Pius IX provided a vivid, if implicit, approbation of the new order when he borrowed (at a substantial rate of interest) some fifty million francs from the Rothschild banking house for remodeling and repairing St. Peter's Basilica. Finally, the whole issue came full circle in the 1983 Code of Canon Law, which said, "All administrators are bound to fulfill their office with the diligence of a good householder.... For this reason they, with the consent of the ordinary, should invest the money which is left over after expenses and which can be profitably allocated for the goals of the juridic person."[13] In other words, that which was formerly deemed intrinsically evil has come to be regarded as a serious moral obligation on the part of Church management.

"SHAPED BY CHRISTIAN EXPERIENCE"

How did the change come about—all in such a short period of time? Within some thirty years (1556–86), moral doctrine taught at the highest levels of the Catholic Church was questioned, undermined, and buried. John Noonan gives special credit to the theologians who cautiously juggled the needs of the times with their respect for Church authority. The task was especially difficult for the Jesuits, who took a special vow of obedience to the pope. The theologians worked their way through the maze in several ways: by assuming that some moral requirements long considered to be of divine origin were, in fact, merely positive, papal laws subject to reconsideration; by making distinctions within the law that the old morality and the popes had not made; by considering exceptions to the law that a wise lawgiver would have considered if fully aware of the facts; by reflecting on the experience and sincere perceptions of those involved in borrowing and lending; and by pondering the theological significance of widespread nonacceptance of the traditional condemnations of usury.

Concludes Noonan,

> Acts of papal authority, isolated from theological support and contrary to the convictions of Christians familiar with the practices condemned, could not prevail, however accurately they reflected the assumptions and traditions of an earlier age. The theologians were to have the last word, because acts of papal authority are inert unless taught by theologians, because those who cared consulted them, because they taught the next generation, and because the very categories in which the papal teaching was put were shaped by Christian experience and theological analysis.[14]

SIX

CATHERINE OF SIENA
"Blind Is the Pastor"

On a pleasant summer evening in the year 1376, a small ship moved slowly, against the stream, up the Rhone River in France. As the ship approached the city of Avignon and the passengers prepared to disembark, they had their first view of the great palace of the popes, situated on a high, rocky bluff overlooking the river. It had been constructed in stages over the previous sixty-five years, which could explain its somewhat odd appearance, as noted by historian Barbara Tuchman:

The palace [was] a huge and inharmonious mass of roofs and towers without coherent design. Constructed in castle style around interior courts, with battlements and twelve-foot-thick walls for defense, it had odd pyramidal chimneys rising from the kitchens, banqueting halls and gardens, money chambers and offices, rose-windowed chapels, a steam room for the Pope heated by a boiler, and a gate opening on the public square where the faithful gathered to watch the Holy Father ride out on his white mule. Here moved the majestic cardinals in their wide red hats...vying with each other in the magnificence of their suites. One required ten stables for his horses, and another rented parts of 51 houses to lodge all his retainers.[1]

The current pontiff, Gregory XI, was the latest of six successive popes, all Frenchmen, who made Avignon their home. And the once small, sleepy town had grown into a city of more than fifty thousand — a vast throng of clergy and other church officials, their assistants, retainers, servants, and the families of these church people. But there were also ambassadors, adventurers, sightseers, artisans, craftsmen, prostitutes, thieves, and bankers — especially bankers. Some fifty-three Italian banking houses had branches there, for money was the largest industry in Avignon, and it was said that one could not enter any of the offices of the palace without encountering brokers and clergy counting and recording the money lying in heaps before them.

The most prominent of those who got off the boat was a twenty-eight-year-old woman wearing the white habit and black veil of the Dominican order and accompanied by a small group of followers, including her secretary, confessor, and best friend, Raymond of Capua. She was Catherine of Siena, and she had acquired in her short life a considerable reputation as mystic and wonder worker.

Petrarch, a poet of the time, called Avignon the "Babylon of the West," a place of licentious banquets and obscene luxury for the chosen, contrasting with the grime, poverty, and disgusting smells wafting through the narrow streets of the lower classes. Reportedly, Catherine could "smell" serious sin when she encountered it, and Raymond reported that she almost suffocated from the stench as she entered the city. But she had not come to sniff out sin among the thieves and money collectors. She came to Avignon to work a wonder. Catherine was certain that Christ called her there to confront Pope Gregory, to do as St. Paul had done in the days of old — to withstand Peter to his face.

A CENTURY GONE WRONG

A peculiar sense of gloom and dread hovered foglike over the entire fourteenth century and permeated most of its events. All at once, it seemed, nature itself had turned hostile to humanity, civilization had lost its moorings, and even the Holy Spirit had deserted the Church. Foundations crumbled, and no one knew what lay in the future except chaos. Avignon, with its wretched excess of wealth on the one hand and its miserable poverty on the other, came to symbolize everything that had gone wrong.

The trouble in nature started early in the century's first decade. Unseasonably cold winters heralded the start of what came to be known as the "Little Ice Age," a climatic shift that would last for almost four hundred years. In 1315 crops failed all over in Europe, and sporadic failures continued into the 1620s and 1630s, resulting in starvation in some regions, general malnourishment, and the uprooting of many rural communities.

That upheaval was nothing compared to the arrival in Sicily of the Black Plague. It came on a ship of sick and dying sailors from the Crimea in 1347, and no one would discover how to stop it for another five hundred years. In a three-year sweep through almost every section of the Continent and British Isles, it wiped out an estimated twenty million people, one-third of Europe's population. The bacillus, spread mostly by fleas and rats, killed so quickly that some people went to bed feeling healthy and died before dawn. Doctors tending patients sometimes succumbed at bedside while the patients lingered on. Crowded cities were the hardest hit. Paris lost half its population, and so did Avignon. Florence, just recovering from a famine, lost three-fourths of its people to the plague. In Britain, during one twelve-month period, the archbishop of Canterbury died, as did his successor and the successor of the successor. During the next sixty years there would be six additional lesser epidemics of the plague.

Perhaps more frightful was the effect of so much death on the survivors. It seemed to many that God had given up on his creation, as he did in the days of Noah. Some threw up their hands, abandoning themselves to debauchery and crime; others sought to appease the divinity through extravagant penances and mortification; still others decided that the Jews caused the plague by poisoning wells or spreading disease in little packages that they distributed in public places. Major pogroms occurred all over Europe. In some cities, Strasbourg and Brussels, for example, whole Jewish populations were wiped out.

Meanwhile, the fourteenth century was torn by continuous political wars, rebellions, and uprisings. Hardly a year of the century passed without a broken treaty and the outbreak of more violence. It was just in the middle of the century — as the last plague victims were being laid to rest—that the record-setting Hundred Years War between France and England broke out, a nonstop slaughter that continued for four generations.

The Church's problems likewise began early in the century, when Philip the Fair of France began taxing Church income without the permission of Pope Boniface VIII. The pope prepared to excommunicate Philip, so in 1303 Philip's forces seized the eighty-six-year-old pope at his summer home near Rome and held him captive, intending to bring him to trial for crimes ranging from simony and sodomy to harboring a small pet demon in the papal quarters. Italian citizens managed to liberate Boniface, but he died a month later due to ill treatment during the abduction. The newly elected pope, Clement V, a French native, refused to go to Rome, lest he be attacked by the French-hating, revenge-seeking Roman population. Consequently, he settled down in Avignon, a beautiful, peaceable city near the mouth of the Rhone.

Here Clement and the next six popes concentrated on two things: first, the centralization of their authority over every aspect of Church business, including the appointment of bishops, the granting of dispensations and indulgences, and the conferring of honors; second, the acquisition of huge, unprecedented amounts of money through the taxation of every one of the centralized activities of Church government. Money was required for the ongoing construction of the new papal compound, for the pope's army in its defense of the troubled Papal States, as well as for the burgeoning prodigality of everyday life at Avignon. Corruption among clergy at the top fostered corruption at the bottom, which in turn fostered resentment among the laity. It was the laity at the local level, of course, who ultimately had to supply the funds that were pushed up the pipeline to the top. No one knew how to stop the pattern of corruption.

MYSTICS AND SEERS

Catherine of Siena came to Avignon to enforce God's judgment, to rouse the Church (and with it all society) out of the depressing paralysis of the times. Wide-ranging Church reform had to be carried out, she believed, and that would not happen until Gregory departed from this Babylon of the West and went back where the popes belonged. Some argued that it made no difference where the Church maintained its headquarters. For Catherine it was a life-and-death issue: in leaving Rome, the Church had abandoned the blood and bones of its martyrs, the resting place of Peter and Paul; it had preferred ease and luxury over commitment and the cross. She did not intend to allow that situation to endure.

Catherine had no claim to wisdom or authority other than her conviction that God spoke through her and demanded compliance now. Yet, in the agitated fourteenth century, such a claim did not seem as bizarre as it might today. For if there were extremes in nature, state, and church, there were equally extremes in the practice of spirituality. These extremes, manifested in a host of fourteenth-century mystics, were rarely disparaged; they gave shreds of hope to common folk and they induced a bit of fear in the mighty. Maybe God had not totally abandoned creation after all. People were fascinated by the likes of Julian of Norwich, Henry Suso, Dorothy of Montau, Margery Kempe, and others, whom Richard Kieckhefer discusses in his book *Unquiet Souls: Fourteenth-Century Saints and Their Religious Milieu.* They were similar, he notes, in extraordinary patience, their acceptance (almost enjoyment) of suffering, their proclivity for visions and revelations from the other world, their devotion to (and sometimes obsession with) the details of Christ's passion and death, and their insistence that one should not seek or expect much in the way of joy or personal fulfillment in this world.

Only two of these remarkable people, notes Kieckhefer, presumed to enter the public arena, criticize leaders of church or state, and tell them in the plainest terms that they were wrong. The two were Bridget of Sweden and Catherine of Siena. They never met (Bridget died at seventy, three years before Catherine's arrival in Avignon), and it is doubtful that either was more than vaguely aware of the other's activities. Yet, strangely enough, they shared nearly identical agendas.

Bridget, a cousin of the king of Sweden, married at thirteen into another aristocratic family and had eight children before her husband, Ulf, died. She then transformed herself into a "bride of Christ" and launched a new life as combination contemplative and woman of action. She started a religious order of women (the Brigittines), admonished bishops and royalty in Sweden, then swooped down into

Rome in 1349. There, speaking in the name of Jesus, Mary, and various saints, she called for massive Church reform — above all, the return of the pope to Rome. In the pope's absence, the eternal city had come on hard times.

> Dependent formerly on the immense business of the papal court, Rome had no thriving commerce like that of Florence or Venice to fall back on. In the absence of the papacy it had sunk into poverty and chronic disorder; the population dwindled from over 50,000 before the Black Death to 20,000; classical monuments, tumbled by earthquake or neglect, were vandalized for their stones; cattle were stabled in abandoned churches, streets were pitted with stagnant pools and strewn with rubbish. Rome had no poets like Dante and Petrarch, ... no university like Paris and Bologna, no flourishing studios of painting and sculpture. It did harbor one notable, holy figure, Brigitta of Sweden, who was kind and meek to every creature, but a passionate denouncer of the corruption of the hierarchy.[2]

Due in large part to Bridget's letters, prayers, and arousal of public opinion over an eighteen-year period in Rome, Pope Urban VI in 1367 left Avignon amid much weeping. Only a handful of sad cardinals accompanied him to Rome, and many of the Church's administrative offices remained in the French city. His stay was brief. Lured by siren songs from Avignon and overwhelmed by the miserable conditions of Rome and the ceaseless wars and rebellions in the Papal States, Urban never settled in. In 1370, when he announced his return to Avignon, Bridget lashed out in the voice of Mary the Mother of God:

> As a mother leads her child where she will ... so I led him to Rome by my prayers. What does he now do? He turns his back on me ... and would leave me. ... For it wearies him to do his duty, and he is longing for ease and comfort ... for his own country, and his carnally minded friends. ... If he should succeed in getting back to his own country, he will be struck such a blow that his teeth will shake in his mouth, his sight will be darkened and all his limbs will tremble ... and he will be called to account to God for what he did and what he did not do.[3]

It is uncertain whether Urban received this message before departing. In any event, his stay in Avignon was short lived too. He contracted a fever and died within a month of his return. (Apparently, Mary's anger with Urban was also somewhat short lived; he was declared blessed by Pope Pius IX in 1870.)

"BE A MAN, FATHER"

Now, six years later, it was Catherine's turn, this time face-to-face with Urban's successor, Gregory XI. Though she lacked the royal blood and maturity of Bridget, she fairly glowed with charisma. She was the twenty-third of twenty-four children born to Lappa and Giacomo Benincasa of Siena. (The last child, Catherine's twin sister, died shortly after birth.) Giacomo was a wool dyer by trade, and except for sheer numbers, the family was not otherwise exceptional — until Catherine arrived. At age five she had a vision of SS. Peter and Paul and Jesus (wearing the papal tiara). At six she ran away from home with a loaf of bread and hid in a cave outside town, intending to become a hermit. At seven she pledged herself to Christ as his bride for life. She began to experience visions and frequent ecstasies, becoming rigid and unconscious; on one such occasion she fell into a burning fireplace, from which she was quickly extricated without injury.

She remained in her room praying for long periods. When she was twelve, her concerned parents demanded that she come out, live a normal life, and start thinking about marriage. She informed them of her betrothal to Christ and would yield to neither argument nor pressure. If she could not remain in her room, she would create a "secret cell...not of stone or wood but of self-knowledge" in which to dwell. Her parents ceased the pressure only after her father one day observed a dove hovering over Catherine as she knelt in prayer. Christ, he acknowledged, might not be such a bad son-in-law after all.

· During her teen years Catherine was enrolled as a tertiary (third order) Dominican, a group composed for the most part of widows who pledged themselves to celibacy and charitable works and who were permitted to wear the order's habit though not confined to convent life or discipline. At twenty she told of a vision in which Christ formalized her betrothal and gave her a ring and a special garment visible only to herself. He also gave her a kiss that, she said, filled her with "unutterable sweetness." Henceforth, Christ required her to go into the world. She immediately became as outgoing and gregarious as she had been previously withdrawn. She visited the sick, cheered the depressed, counseled the quarreling, converted sinners, and gave advice to young and old. Her feats of self-denial became legendary; it was said she was unable to consume any food but the Eucharist in her adult life and permitted herself less than an hour of sleep a night. During a recurrence of the Black Plague, in which six of her nieces and nephews died, she tended the sick night and day. She was credited with bringing some terminal patients back to health.

Gradually, Catherine attracted a retinue of devoted followers who spread stories of her works and visions throughout Siena and beyond. She called them "dearest family"; they called her "Mamma." Scholars have since wondered at the sheer volume of reports about her effect on throngs of people in such a short period of time. Writes Carol Lee Flinders,

> The stories are so many and so convergent — of hardened sinners or world-weary skeptics who had only to come into her presence to fall down sobbing and go off to confession immediately, their lives profoundly and permanently reversed. Her power to do this seems to have had everything to do with the way she looked at you, the enormous interest and understanding that glowed out her huge, dark eyes. There would come a day when she was criticized severely for permitting people to fall onto their knees in her presence. She looked blank and then laughed, "I am so busy reading their souls that I have no idea what is happening to their bodies!"[4]

In 1374, when she was twenty-seven, Catherine went into a deep ecstatic state — a mystic death — then came out of it with the announcement that Christ now commanded her to move into the wider world of church and state. For much of the time during the six remaining years of her life, she was on the road — to Florence, to Pisa, to Rome — speaking to ever growing crowds, working miracles, meeting with Church leaders and government officials, carrying on a massive correspondence. Continually, she sought to bring peace and order to the violence-prone Papal States. In several instances she acted as the semi-official papal spokesman in Florence. Before she came to Avignon, she wrote direct, even quaintly affectionate, letters to the pope, though the recurring message could not be ignored:

> He who loves himself, be he a prelate or subordinate, cannot do anything but evil and all virtue is dead in him. He is like a woman who brings forth dead children.... Woe, woe, sweetest Babbo mio! This is the reason why all the subordinates are corrupted in impurity and injustice.... Blind are the sick who do not know their own disease, and blind is the pastor who ought to be the healer, but who never dares to use either the knife of justice or the fire of true love.[5]

In later letters she grew more practical and specific: "There are three things which God requires of you. The first is to reform the Church — to pull up the bad herbs by the roots, that is to say, the bad pastors and governors who poison and corrupt the garden, and to cast them outside."[6]

The second was to come to Rome: "Be a man. Father, arise! No negligence! Do God's will and mine!... I am persuaded that if only you know the needs of the Church you will do it [abandon Avignon] with no fear or negligence. The soul which fears men will never wholly achieve anything, it will fail everywhere and finish nothing.... I am begging you.... I am telling you!"[7]

The third requirement was that Gregory organize a crusade to free the Holy Land from the Saracens. The papal military armies at that time were in regular combat with the revolutionary forces in the Papal States. Catherine was convinced that the fighting would cease if only the pope could find another, more distant enemy: "Therefore I pray you sweetly, since you delight so much in making war and fighting, make no more war upon Christians because it offends God."[8]

Pope Gregory had been receiving such letters for several years, and though he indicated at various times that he thought of going to Rome, he had never made a single move in that direction until Catherine arrived on his doorstep.

MISSION ACHIEVED

Her audience with the pope occurred on June 20, 1376, in the great Gothic hall at Avignon, he on the papal throne, she standing before him speaking in the Tuscan Italian accent of her home and pausing intermittently while Raymond of Capua translated her message into Latin. (The French pope understood not a word of Italian.) The dialogue between the two was not transcribed, but the substance of Catherine's message could be summarized from her later comments and other sources: The pope must begin reform immediately by appointing worthy leaders all over Christendom. He must pacify Italy not by bloodshed but by mercy and pardon. He must return to Rome not with an armed guard but with the cross in his hand. She ended with, "For it seems to me that Divine Goodness is preparing to change furious wolves into lambs—and I will bring them humiliated to your bosom....O Father, peace for the love of God!"⁹

What Gregory said in reply is not known. But, as subsequent events indicated, he was torn apart by her visit. It seemed to inspire in him, noted one of her biographers, "a sort of terror....[He] felt the consuming will burning in that slight woman; in her glowing love of Jesus she willed, willed, *willed* to conform all to her dearly loved Spouse."

Still, he vacillated, authorizing three theologians to interview Catherine to determine the orthodoxy of this prophet. It was reported that they quizzed her aggressively about her visions and fasting, referred to her as "a wretched little female," and concluded with a reminder that the children of darkness are quite adept at disguising themselves as children of light. Nevertheless, she passed the exam. If she hadn't, noted the pope's physician, she certainly would have been handed over to the Inquisition.

At last Gregory announced that he had made up his mind; he was packing up—no more delays—and would depart shortly for Rome. Immediately, he was overwhelmed with argument and resistance from the whole papal court. Why abandon the peace of Avignon for the dangers of a city engaged in war? Why leave his French supporters for a people who despised the French? Catherine kept informed of these developments and bombarded the pope with letters, lest his resolve falter: "And I say to you in the name of Christ Crucified that you have no cause whatsoever for fear. Be of good courage and depart in Christ Jesus.... Be a man, Father, arise!... And if there be some who would hinder you, then say to them what Christ said to Peter: 'Get behind me, Satan!' "

The cardinals threatened mutiny, and a highly regarded Franciscan informed the pope that a plot was already afoot in Rome to poison him on arrival. Catherine, in a fiery note to Gregory, called the Franciscan an "incarnate demon," adding that "there is probably just as much poison in Avignon as in Rome, and such things can be bought everywhere."

Finally, reluctantly, painfully, Gregory made the move. On September 13, three months after Catherine's arrival, he came out of the palace gate for the last time. The cardinals and court officials burst into tears, and the pope's aged father fell on the ground to block the way. Gregory stepped politely over him and continued on, reciting a psalm.

The pope's ship ran into storms as it journeyed along the Mediterranean, and there were long delays at various ports. At Genoa he received word that Roman citizens were rioting against the papacy, and his advisors told him it would be suicidal to proceed farther. The pope became despondent and nearly did turn back. But as fate would have it, Catherine was staying in Genoa at the time. So the desperate Gregory, alone and dressed like a simple priest, went to see her one night to explain how the situation had changed, to seek her permission to return to Avignon, at least for a time. The visit lasted through the night. In the morning the pope returned to the ship, reportedly "strengthened and edified," determined to forge on to Rome regardless of consequences.

When he did get there, the revolt was over and he was received joyfully. Awaiting him was a letter from Catherine: "Ah, Babbo, no more war; imitate the Lamb without blemish.... I trust He will work this in you and fulfill His will and mine."[10]

Gregory did make efforts at reform, but he was continuously preoccupied with the uprisings in the Papal States. More importantly, he had only fifteen months to live in Rome before he was stricken with a fever and died quite suddenly at the age of fifty.

The Babylonian exile was over at last and the long-awaited reform would come — but not right away. First, the Church had to endure a bewildering, thirty-six-year period called the "Western Schism" —

with two, and eventually three, contenders for the papal throne. Catherine herself lived only long enough to witness the early stages of the schism. "Do not weep," she told Raymond of Capua, "for you will have still more to weep for."[11]

She continued her public ministry for two more years. Then, in 1380, following a dreamlike vision in which she felt the weight of the whole Church — like a great ship pressing on her back — she collapsed in paralysis and died soon after. She was thirty-three years old.

Ever since, countless biographers have puzzled over this blessedly eccentric woman, this product of the feverish fourteenth century who knew, better than the pope, what the good of the Church required, who did not fear to move mountains to achieve her goal. And ever since, the Church has never hesitated to extol her greatness. Catherine of Siena was canonized in 1461, was named (along with Francis of Assisi) the copatron saint of Italy in 1939, and was declared a doctor of the Church in 1970.

SEVEN

MATTEO RICCI
An Open Door to China

During a remarkably productive ten years in the middle of the sixteenth century, the Jesuit missionary Francis Xavier converted an estimated one million persons to Christianity. In India, Indonesia, and Japan, he had unparalleled success in preaching the gospel. Yet, wherever he went, someone would inevitably pose an intriguing objection: "If yours is the true faith, why have not the Chinese, from whom comes all wisdom, heard of it?" And so toward the end of his life, Xavier made a valiant effort to bring his message to the immense, sprawling Middle Kingdom, as the Chinese referred to their land. His effort was in vain. The missionary died in 1552 on a small island off the coast of China, still attempting to persuade ship owners to give him passage to the great country. None dared, because the Chinese government had imposed a policy of extreme isolationism for more than a hundred years. The Ming emperors viewed their country as situated at the middle of the earth, threatened on all sides by barbarians ignorant of the wisdom and culture flourishing in this land. Contact with foreign traders or foreign ambassadors was always limited, always temporary, and always on terms greatly to China's advantage. Contact with promoters of foreign religion was forbidden.

For two decades after Xavier's death Franciscan and Dominican missionaries tried to gain a foothold in China, only to be similarly denied access. Then quite suddenly in the latter years of the sixteenth century a breakthrough was achieved — both into the country itself and into the culture and traditions of China. Jesuit missionaries, using innovative approaches that departed radically from established Catholic procedures of the time, created a kind of Chinese-Catholicism that seemed destined to bring millions into the Church. But in fact, the approach was destined to failure, not so much because of resistance from inside China but because of sustained resistance from European churchmen.

A CATHOLIC MANDARIN

In 1577, twenty-five years after Xavier's death, Alessandro Valignano, the new director of Jesuit activities in the East, arrived on the island of Macao, a tiny spit of rock connected to the Chinese mainland by a narrow causeway. Here Portuguese traders and government officials had established a small town with the permission of China, and from here all access to the kingdom was strictly controlled. Like Francis Xavier before him, Valignano wanted no part of the conquest-and-convert pattern that the Spanish and Portuguese were employing in the Americas. There the conquistadors would announce to the native peoples that their land had been "discovered" and turned over to the European powers by the Church. In the Caribbean islands, the so-called *Requiremento* informed the subjugated natives (in Spanish), "His Holiness Alexander VI has donated these isles of Terra Firma to the kings of Spain." If they failed to cooperate, "We shall take you and your wives and your children and shall sell and dispose of you however their highnesses may command. And we shall take away your goods and shall do all the harm and damage that we can."[1]

Asia was simply too big for such massive conquest, a fact Valignano regarded as a blessing. Conversion to the Catholic faith would come freely in this part of the world or not at all. He brought to Macao several younger Jesuits and set them to work learning the Chinese language and its culture. One of these, Michele Ruggieri, was allowed on occasion to travel to the mainland to say Mass for Portuguese traders. On one of his trips Ruggieri acted as a mediator and translator for a group of Franciscan missionaries who had landed illegally in China and were being prosecuted. Officials in the city of Zhaoqing were so taken with Ruggieri's knowledge of Chinese, his respectful demeanor, and his awareness of local customs that in 1582 they allowed him to set up a small residence in the city — an unprecedented event. He was accompanied on this venture by a thirty-year-old Italian Jesuit who had been preparing for such an opportunity on Macao, Matteo Ricci.

When Ruggieri shortly afterwards returned to Europe, Ricci became director of Jesuit activities on the mainland while reporting to Valignano on Macao. From that point on Ricci's experiences were so dramatic and unexpected that they could well form the plot of a multipart television series.

At first, Ricci shaved his head and beard, dressed like a Buddhist, and immersed himself in the life of Zhaoqing. He became an object of great curiosity. Taking his home to be a Buddhist gathering place, people stopped in at all hours of day or night to discuss philosophy with this strange man from the West. Such was his hospitality that word spread, and visitors began to arrive from far away to stay for protracted periods in his house. Amid his duties as host, cook, and conversationalist, Matteo Ricci was soaking up great amounts of information about Chinese culture and religion. Ricci had on the wall of his house a map of the world that fascinated his visitors. They were amazed and somewhat taken aback to learn that China was positioned on the far right of the map with Europe in the center. Ricci then skillfully redrew the map, inserting Chinese characters and placing China, the Middle Kingdom, in the middle of the map. This edited version was published and copies distributed widely.

Since Confucianism was the official doctrine of China, Ricci soon decided he could make greater progress if he adopted the style and manner of a Confucian scholar. So he let his hair and beard grow and traded his Buddhist robes for the silk garments of the educated literati who studied the doctrines of the great master. This was a daring move because the teachings of Confucius were exceedingly complex, not easily mastered even by those fluent in the Mandarin tongue. One who pretended learning in this area faced instant rebuke and dishonor; a pretender from outside could anticipate deportation or worse. But Ricci set himself to the task of becoming fluent in the language, conquering the basic texts, even translating them into Latin for Valignano's benefit.

Confucius, who lived some five hundred years before Christ, developed a moral code and lifestyle based on seeking righteousness and truth. The supreme virtue (*Jen*), much like magnanimity or love or even charity, placed great emphasis on filial piety — honoring family members and ancestors. The system lacked a developed theology but was quite supportive of religious practice. Ricci began to think that within the doctrine of Confucius, as found in his famous *Four Books* and *Five Classics,* resided an ethical-philosophical system amazingly compatible with Christianity.

In order to advance in Chinese society, students had to pass a series of stringent exams in Confucian thought. Those who passed joined the select company of the literati or mandarins, and only such persons were eligible for administrative positions in the government. Access to the exams, however, was available to anyone from any level of society. As a result, governmental corruption was minimal, since both job opportunity and advancement were related to proven intellectual ability, not to caste or to connections with people in high places.

Ricci's ability to master Confucian thought proved phenomenal. In a relatively short time he not only understood the basic texts and other works, he memorized much of the material — in Mandarin Chinese. Consequently, he was invited everywhere and went everywhere. In one conversation over dinner with a group of distinguished scholars, he reportedly dazzled the guests with his ability to recite whole passages from the classics (given to him at random) and to repeat instantly, forward or backward, lists of characters from the mammoth Chinese alphabet.

More importantly, Ricci's manner was exceptionally personable, outgoing, disarming — despite his prodigious knowledge. He seemed able to create trust and develop lasting friendships with scores of the people he encountered. He began to be addressed affectionately by his Chinese name, Li Madou, and within a few years scattered literati began to enter the Church.

Some historians have claimed that this very bright Jesuit won the favor of the literati through his knowledge of physics and astronomy and especially with the various Western inventions he brought to China,

most notably, clocks. But most have concluded that few Chinese —
and none of the literati — would have taken him seriously if he had not
demonstrated beforehand great astuteness in the classics. According to
historian Andrew Ross,

> He believed that without gaining a foothold in that class [the
> literati] and thereby winning a general toleration for the Soci-
> ety [the Jesuits] and its mission by that class as a whole, there
> was no way in which Chinese missionary presence could operate
> with any hope of success in China. Before the mass of common-
> ers would be reached on any significant scale the Society had to
> establish itself as a part of Chinese society, and that was only pos-
> sible with at least the acquiescence, if not the active support of
> the literati.[2]

THE ROAD TO PEKING

Valignano and Ricci both believed that long-range success would require some form of permission for Jesuit presence in China from the
supreme emperor in Peking, the capital. And it was in his efforts
to achieve this that Ricci met considerable frustration. One attempt
to reach Peking by horseback and barge ended tragically when the
barge capsized in dangerous rapids and Ricci's young Jesuit compan-
ion drowned. Ricci, himself a nonswimmer, clung to a rope and was
rescued. Nevertheless, the failed journey provided new opportunities.
He was forced on his way back to stay for several months in the city
of Nanchang. Here he learned that the name and reputation of his
Chinese alias, Li Madou, had preceded him. He was feted by the
provincial, viceroy, and members of the imperial family. Here he established another house, formed the first, small community of converts
to Catholicism, and wrote his first work in the Mandarin tongue, *A
Treatise on Friendship.* This commentary on the Confucian classics became a kind of best-seller and a classic in its own right, much revered
even long after Ricci's time. Also in Nanchang he learned of the opposition to his approach on the part of so-called Neo-Confucians —
those who promoted a decidedly atheistic, materialistic interpretation
of the Confucian texts.

A second attempt to reach Peking proved successful, but here Ricci and his party were confronted with strong antiforeign antagonism from the eunuchs who manned the imperial palace. Access to the Forbidden City, the emperor's dwelling place, was denied, and on their way back, Ricci and his associates nearly perished in the winter cold. But again, Ricci's resilience prevailed. Stranded for a time in the city of Nanjing, the southern capital of the empire, he made friends with the imperial censor, a man of exceptional authority in the Chinese bureaucracy.

In 1600 the censor graciously provided Ricci and three other Jesuits with passports to the capital, along with letters of introduction. Arriving in Peking, the missionaries were warmly greeted by the scholarly community. But an especially aggressive eunuch overseer, Ma Tang, jailed the foreigners and confiscated the gifts they brought for the emperor. They languished in prison for five months under various threats — including life imprisonment or death — while their literati friends, including the minister of rites, the secretary of the board of personnel, and even the grand secretary, struggled to overturn Ma's domination.

Meanwhile, the palace eunuchs were totally baffled by the gifts they had seized, in particular a clavichord and several chiming clocks. Ever resourceful, Ricci offered to provide instruction. And so, still a prisoner, he was allowed entrance to the Forbidden City, where he explained clock usage and maintenance. One of his companions showed the eunuchs how to play the clavichord, even composing several songs, much to their delight. (Apparently, music was one of the few skills that Ricci lacked.) When the emperor viewed the clocks, he was taken with their beauty, but the ultimate release of the Jesuits was due to the intercession of Ricci's old friend, the imperial censor.

Although they were never permitted to meet the emperor, the Jesuits were allowed — to Ricci's delight — to set up a residence in the capital and to function freely in the city. He had achieved what he came for: a legitimate presence in the seat of Chinese culture and tacit permission to engage publicly in missionary work.

A MEETING OF JESUS AND CONFUCIUS

The years from 1600 to 1610 proved the most productive in Ricci's life. Spending most of his time in Peking, writing and conferring with scholars, he developed more fully his ideas on a happy marriage between Catholicism and Confucianism. Of singular importance was how to understand God. And in those times a significant difference existed between the Neo-Confucian view and that of the more traditional Confucian scholars with whom Ricci agreed. In the classical sense the word *tian* meant "heaven," and *shangdi* was understood as "lord on high" — the one to whom sacrifices were offered in centuries past. Ricci argued (with elaborate references to the classics) that Confucius regarded both terms as referring to a personal, creator God, a rewarder of good and punisher of evil; as such, they were equivalent to the "God" words in the Bible. The Neo-Confucians, who interpreted these terms impersonally, as "the heavens above" or "the order of reality," were simply wrong, asserted Ricci, and disrespectful of tradition as well.

Ricci also wrestled with the very delicate, time-honored practice of offering prayers and sacrifices to the deceased on the occasion of funerals and on other specified days throughout the year. Also deeply ingrained were yearly sacrificial ceremonies in honor of Confucius himself. After much reading and writing on the subject, Ricci concluded that in their original context these rites were expressions of deep love for the deceased along with a conviction that their souls had moved on into another world. If these rites had become shot through with superstition for some, if Confucius was regarded as a kind of divinity by others, if the ceremonies were empty civic rituals for still others — all that, said Ricci, amounted to unfortunate accretion. Similar excesses regarding veneration of the faithful departed were not unknown in Catholic Europe. Thus, he concluded, Catholic Chinese converts could engage in ancestral rites, provided they interpreted them in an orthodox manner; he still maintained some doubts about the annual Confucian sacrifices and advised literati converts to abstain.

On a host of other customs he endeavored to place a Christian understanding or at least a harmless interpretation. For example, the *kou tou,* a traditional practice of bowing deeply or kneeling before an important person, was a gesture of respect in Confucian teaching, said Ricci, and should not be confused with genuflection, an act of adoration. And the small tablets dedicated to deceased relatives and kept in special places in homes should not be considered as actually containing the souls of relatives (as some believed), argued Ricci, and were never so considered in original Confucian teaching.

In what is perhaps his most important book, *On the True Meaning of the Lord of Heaven,* Ricci made a supreme effort to inculturate Christianity in a non-European system. The doctrines of the creed were to be presented clearly but always adapted to the sensitivities of Chinese history and culture. In a very real sense, his biographers have noted, Ricci tried to do for Confucius what Thomas Aquinas did for Aristotle: provide a complex belief system with a philosophical and moral undergirding, thus making the mysteries of the faith more approachable to the people of a specific culture.

His work constituted a very original and radical interpretation of the Christian message, and it was all achieved over a period of about fifteen years with virtually no input from Rome. On several occasions Valignano contacted Jesuit and papal authorities, but more to inform Church officials what was going on than to seek permission. Ironically, at the very time of this adaptation in China, the requirements of the Council of Trent (concluded less than twenty years before Ricci's arrival in China) were being imposed throughout the world. In its effort to weed out heresies, Trent attached specific, unchangeable meanings to dogmas and doctrines; even minor variances were forbidden under pain of mortal sin, and participation in non-Christian ceremonies was unthinkable. So technically, the Jesuits in China were far out of line with Roman practice.

Yet clearly, Ricci and his associates believed that they were justified in bending the rules and canons; they had been sent, as the Jesuit constitution stated, "to seek the greater glory of God and the good of souls whether among the faithful or the infidels." Besides, it required upwards of four years to send a letter from the Far East to Europe and receive a reply, and everyone knew that this window of opportunity might close at any time.

Ricci was fifty-eight years old in 1610 when he fell ill quite suddenly and died within eleven days. By order of the emperor his body lay in state in Peking while hundreds of mandarins plus a throng of curious Chinese commoners paid their respects. It was then ceremoniously carried to a special tomb near the western gate of the imperial city. The plaque read:

To one who loved righteousness and wrote illustrious books,
To *Li Madou,* Far Westerner.[3]

Matteo Ricci left behind fewer than five hundred converts in all of
China, but he had never seen his task as personally converting the
masses. Reportedly, his last words to his Jesuit friends were, "I leave
you facing an open door."[4]

A CENTURY OF GROWTH

And the door would remain open for more than a hundred years, despite
unpredictable cycles of favor and disfavor, oppression and approval.
Records of the Catholic population in those years are estimates at best,
yet all indicate constant growth. In 1613 the number was placed at 5,000;
in 1627 it had grown to 13,000; in 1650 it increased more than tenfold
to 150,000; in 1667, 162,000. By the end of the century the estimated
number of Chinese Catholics ranged from 250,000 to half a million.

Three years after Ricci's death, his successor, Nicolo Longobordo,
sent a representative to Rome to gather support for the work and possibly to gain some official approval of Confucian Christianity. The
emissary, Nicolo Trigault, succeeded in obtaining permission from
Pope Paul V for celebrants at Mass in China to wear the traditional
ceremonial headgear; permission was also granted for Chinese priests
to celebrate Mass in the vernacular. However, there were no Chinese
priests at the time, nor would there be until late in the century, due to
political upheaval and communication problems between China and
Rome. To what extent Trigault discussed with Vatican officials the full
implications of Ricci's adaptations is not known.

Meanwhile, Longobordo benefited immensely when the Jesuits
were asked to take over the work of preparing the imperial calendar
and overseeing the bureau of astronomy. It was the astronomers' duty
to plot the movement of stars and planets throughout each year and to
accurately predict any extraordinary celestial phenomena. These positions carried huge prestige, and news of the appointments spread
rapidly through the empire. The Jesuits were to hold these posts during
most of the seventeenth century, and their work resulted in constant
publicity, frequent honor, and large amounts of grief.

In such highly visible roles, the Jesuits became subject to the chronic hostility directed at foreigners; they were sometimes accused of consorting with the subversive terrorist organization the White Lotus Society, and sometimes charged with using unacceptable scientific methods. On one notable occasion they were challenged to a public contest to test their astronomical skills regarding an expected solar eclipse. Certain Mohammedan scientists predicted the eclipse at 2:30 in the afternoon; selected Chinese experts set the time as 3:00, and the Jesuit astronomers opted for 3:45. As a great gathering of officials at the imperial observatory craned their necks at the sky, nothing happened at 2:30 or at 3:00. Then, at the very instant of 3:45, the shadow of eclipse began to pass across the sun. Many, especially the Jesuits and their literati supporters, cheered, while some claimed that the foreign devils had rigged the event through sorcery.

On another occasion, a crackdown on Christian missionaries was ordered, and Adam Schell, the capable director of missionary operations in China at midcentury, was sentenced to death, along with other Jesuit leaders. But after a devastating earthquake struck Peking, killing three hundred thousand and leveling most of the city, the judges reconsidered and released all the prisoners.

Never in the hundred years were the missionaries without some unforeseen turmoil, especially when the old Ming dynasty was overthrown by Manchu warriors. From every calamity they made notable comebacks, and the Chinese Catholic Church continually developed along the lines proposed by Ricci, with no major internal problems.

OBJECTIONS AND CONTRADICTIONS

But what neither eclipse nor earthquake nor Neo-Confucian agitation could do, challenges from other Catholic missionaries inside China and in Europe did accomplish. During the 1630s a leading Spanish Dominican, Juan Bautista de Morales, drew up a list of objections concerning the Jesuit approach to conversion: first, the missionaries did not insist on observance of the Church's positive precepts, such as the ban against work on Sundays and Holy Days of Obligation; second, they were allowing forbidden, ambiguous terms for God, soul, saint, and so forth; third, they permitted converts to continue their pagan rites of honoring the dead. These accusations Morales submitted to the newly formed Congregation of Propaganda in Rome. And when he failed to get a satisfactory response, he traveled to Rome himself, armed with additional evidence, including Jesuit failure to emphasize the details of Christ's crucifixion, their blatant omission of certain required ceremonies when baptizing women, and their refusal to inform converts that Confucius was in hell.

In lengthy, written responses, the Jesuits attempted to defend their inculturation of Christianity. Positive Church law must always be adapted to circumstances, they said; the anointing of the five senses in the baptism ceremony for women was omitted because Chinese custom permitted only a husband to touch a woman's body; the various Chinese religious terms could be and were understood in a Christian sense; and no one knows whether Confucius or anyone else is in hell.

After long delays the Holy Office in Rome ruled in 1645: henceforth, the Chinese Catholics could not take part in the ancestral rites or in those honoring Confucius; other matters were left untouched. The Jesuits appealed the ruling, sending a representative, Martino Martini, to Rome to defend their position. This resulted in a Holy Office ruling of 1656, which said yes, Christians could practice ancestral rites as long as the Christian interpretation was made very clear.

Seeing an obvious contradiction in these two edicts, the Dominicans and Franciscans sought a clarification, which came in 1669. Both rulings were binding, said the Holy Office! In the view of the Jesuits, this meant that the final decision on allowing or disallowing the rites remained in the hands of the missionaries in the field. They were further encouraged by an Instruction released by the Congregation for Propaganda, which advised missionaries,

> Do not in any way persuade these people to change their customs, their habits and their behaviour; as long as they are not evidently contrary to religion and morality. What could be more absurd, indeed, than to transport France, Italy or some other European country to the Chinese? . . . There exists no more powerful motive for hatred and revulsion than changing ancestral customs, especially those that men have always practised as far back as the memories of their forefathers go.[5]

Still, attacks on the Jesuit methods poured in from Dominican, Franciscan, and other missionaries, all of whom were ministering now in China only because of the goodwill established by the Jesuits. That goodwill was particularly evident in the last decade of the seventeenth century—a hundred years after Ricci's triumph in Peking. In 1692 the emperor published a remarkable edict:

> We have seriously considered the question of the Europeans who ...have crossed the seas....Since they have been living among us they have merited our esteem and gratitude....Since we do not hinder the Bonzes of China from building temples and offering incense to their gods, much less can we forbid these Europeans, who teach only good laws, from having also their churches and preaching their religion publicly in them....All temples dedicated to the Lord of Heaven...ought to be preserved and it is permitted to all...to worship this god....Let no one henceforth offer them any opposition.[6]

Just a few months later a French priest, Charles Maigrot, who had been given the new title of vicar apostolic in China, issued a sweeping "Instruction" that contradicted the validity of everything the Jesuits had done. Confucianism, he ruled, was incompatible with Catholicism, its terms for God could not be used by Christian converts, and its rites were hopelessly flawed with superstition and atheism. As usual, the Jesuits appealed. To strengthen their case, they asked the emperor to explain how he, a Confucian, understood the disputed terms and practices. In effect, he said, Ricci had interpreted the old doctrine accurately. Confucius was considered an honored teacher, not a saint, said the emperor; the rites for the dead were meant to show love of family and ancestors; the house tablets were a remembrance of the dead, not the resting place of their souls; the terms *tian* and *shangdi* referred to a divine being, not an impersonal force. His testimony was submitted to Rome, but Vatican officials did not find his interpretation of his own religion convincing.

THE CLOSING OF THE DOOR

A new, painful era had begun in which Rome grew increasingly involved in every aspect of Confucian Catholicism. The flow of converts ceased, and Christianity became for more than a century a small, un-welcome, persecuted, foreign religion in China. It would never again recover the status it enjoyed in the seventeenth century.

• In 1704 the Holy Office ruled that all the Confucian ceremonies and terms, now long established within the Christian community, could not be interpreted in a Christian sense and were therefore for-bidden. The Roman translators said words like *kou tou, tian,* and *sheng* carried only a pagan or idolatrous sense, and the ancestral rites consti-tuted acts of worship, regardless of how Ricci, the Jesuits in China, or the emperor understood them.

• In 1705 a papal legate, Charles de Tournon, accompanied by Maigrot, had a disastrous meeting with the emperor in Peking. They informed him of the decision of the Holy Office, explaining that the rulings were final and infallible. Appalled by what he regarded as their ignorance of Confucian teaching (not to mention their pitiful grasp of the Chinese language), the emperor said he preferred only the noble Christianity of the great Li Madou. He ordered the expulsion of these ignorant bearers of bad news.

• In 1715 Pope Clement XI issued the bull *Ex Illa Die,* which formalized the condemnations in solemn terms.

• In 1721, as Christianity in China deteriorated, another papal legate, George Mezzabarba, visited the emperor to explain, on sec-ond thought, that concessions might be in order. Some ancestral rites would be permitted under special circumstances, he explained, as well as a modified honoring of Confucius and a quite cautious use of the ancestor tablets. The move was too late, and Ricci's door was about to close. The emperor replied, "Now I have seen the Legate's proclama-tion, and it is just the same as Buddhist...heresies and superstitions. I have never seen such nonsense as this. Henceforth no Westerner may propagate his religion in China. It should be prohibited to avoid more trouble."[7]

• In 1739 Pope Benedict XIV published the bull *Ex Quo Singulari.* It confirmed again the prohibitions of 1704 and laid down a solemn oath to be taken by all missionaries in China:

> I...will fully obey...the apostolic precept and command regard-ing the Rites and Ceremonies of China contained in the Consti-

tution which our Holy Father...has given in this matter...and I will make every effort that this same obedience be rendered by all Chinese Christians....I will never allow the Rites and Ceremonies of China condemned by our Holy Father...to be put into practice by these same Christians....I promise, avow and swear this on the Holy Scriptures.[8]

That oath, which remained in effect for almost two hundred years, was finally abolished in 1938.

The scuttling of the Jesuit endeavor seemed to declare in clear terms that, in the view of the magisterium, there could be no adaptation, no accommodation, no rapprochement between the faith and a "pagan" religion. This position would be echoed in the following centuries, never so clearly as in the writings of Pope Pius IX. Those who see some grace or goodness in non-Christian religions are indifferentists, he said: "With the blurring over of distinctions between virtue and vice, between truth and falsehood, and between goodness and filth, these crafty people pretend that human beings may be saved by practices of [false] religion, as if there could ever be any participation of justice and iniquity, any mixing of light and darkness, and any agreement of Christ with Belial."[9]

But another tradition existed in the Church, one as old as the second century when St. Justin Martyr spoke of the *Logos Spermatikos* — the "Seed of the Word" — as present and operative in the ancient non-Christian religions of his own time. In the twentieth century it was that tradition that would be discussed and developed by missiologists like Johannes Thauren and theologians like Walter Kasper. And it was that tradition that would triumph at the Second Vatican Council:

Other religions to be found everywhere strive variously to answer the restless searchings of the human heart by proposing "ways," which consist of teachings, rules of life, and sacred ceremonies. The Catholic Church rejects nothing which is true and holy in these religions. She looks with sincere respect upon those ways of conduct and life, those rules and teachings which, though differing in many particulars from what she holds and sets forth, nevertheless often reflect a ray of that Truth which enlightens all men.[10]

Christ Himself searched the hearts of men and led them to divine light through truly human conversation. So also His disciples, profoundly penetrated by the Spirit of Christ, should know the people among whom they live and should establish contact with them. Thus they can themselves learn by sincere and patient dialogue what treasures a bountiful God has distributed among the nations of the earth. But at the same time let them try to illumine these treasures with the light of the gospel.... So whatever good is to be found [already] sown in the hearts and minds or in the rites and cultures peculiar to various peoples is not lost.[11]

More recently, Pope John Paul II, in his encyclical *Redemptor hominis,* asked the question, "Does it not sometimes happen that the firm belief of the followers of the non-Christian religions — a belief that is also an effect of the Spirit of truth operating outside the visible confines of the Mystical Body — can make Christians ashamed of being often themselves so disposed to doubt concerning the truths revealed by God?"[12]

It was the kind of question that the great Li Madou — Matteo Ricci — might have asked.

EIGHT

HILDEGARD OF BINGEN
The Feminine Divine

In her own time her works were neither widely read nor well understood. Small wonder! Hildegard of Bingen's teachings on a myriad of topics were so out of harmony with established, unquestioned traditions as to be almost unintelligible. For this was the twelfth century, a time when a convergence of forces had put the pope in a position of absolute control over the Western Church — the beginning of a centuries-long process in which Rome would wield both temporal and spiritual power. It was not a good century for women — a watershed time when two ecumenical councils would dissolve the marriages of all priests, cut adrift their wives and children, and impose a requirement of celibacy on all clerics. Not a good century for anyone — male or female — with novel ideas or imaginative interpretations of old ones.

Yet, here she stood, writing freely and speaking publicly with the full approval of Church authorities, including the pope, almost until her death. Only once did she arouse ecclesiastical wrath, and that was on a rare occasion when she directly challenged the Church's juridical authority. But that incident was a small matter compared with the challenges she presented in a public career of almost forty-three years. Consider some of her positions on theological and scriptural matters:

- In the inner being of God there exists an almost erotic relationship of feminine and masculine that is mirrored in the complementary relationship of men and women.

- Since Jesus took his body from a woman, it is woman rather than man who best represents the humanity of the Son of God.

- Contrary to the clear position of St. Paul, man was made for woman just as equally as woman was made for man.

- In opposition to St. Augustine's doctrine, sexual pleasure is not a result of sin, should not be equated with guilt, and would have been present in Paradise before the Fall.

- Eve was far more the victim of Satan's cunning than the cause of Adam's sin and the fall from grace.

- Menstruation in no way renders a woman unclean, but the shedding of blood in warfare most certainly renders a soldier unclean.

It is almost as if Hildegard were writing for a readership of the future. Indeed, today, some nine hundred years later, she has found a growing audience. Books on her thoughts and doctrine abound, and recordings of her music are popular with secular as well as religious audiences. The internet bookstore amazon.com recently listed some forty-five books currently in print on Hildegard, her theology, or her spirituality — the majority first published in the 1990s.

This is not to suggest that she was unknown in her lifetime; she became, in fact, a genuine celebrity in her later years. Known as the "Sibyl of the Rhine," she carried on a voluminous correspondence with notables of the day (including bishops, theologians, the German emperor Frederic Barbarossa, and King Henry II of England) and with ordinary persons who sought her counsel. She founded two monasteries, which grew to overflowing with candidates; wrote hundreds of hymns and religious songs; answered theological queries; and authored six major books on spirituality and theology and a dozen lesser volumes on gardening, ecology, medicine, and the natural sciences. She also compiled a book of some nine hundred made-up nouns with their German translations. (No one has been able to determine her purpose in this work, titled *Unknown Language,* unless it perhaps provided her with a recreational outlet for her boundless mental energy.) In her sixties and seventies, Hildegard undertook four lengthy and hazardous preaching tours throughout Germany, promoting monastic life and Church reform. Her advice was extremely candid. To an abbess who confided her wish to resign from her duties, Hildegard wrote, "O daughter, born of the side of man and figure formed in the building of God, why do you languish so that your mind shifts like clouds in a storm?... You say, 'I want to rest and seek a place where my soul may rest....' Daughter, it is useless for you to cast off your burden and abandon the flock of God while you have a light to illumine it."[1]

She was even more direct with those who would interfere with the Church. When Barbarossa supported a series of schismatic contenders to the papacy, she scourged him in the name of God almighty: "He who is says, I destroy contumacy, and by myself I crush the resistance of those who despise me. Woe, woe to the malice of wicked men who defy me! Hear this, king, if you wish to live; otherwise my sword shall smite you."[2]

How was she able to attain such prominence in an age that took very literally St. Paul's admonition to Timothy, "No woman is to teach or have authority over a man"?

She did it, first of all, because she was a visionary, not an educated theologian. In the Middle Ages, when women were lightly regarded and little educated, it was only through visions that the insights of an intelligent religious woman would be tolerated. Though never given to ecstasies or trances herself, Hildegard "saw" much of what she wrote about in what she called "the reflection of the Living Light." From early childhood even into her latter years, she said, "My soul, as God would have it, rises up high into the vault of heaven and into the changing sky and spreads itself out among different peoples.... I do not hear them with my outward ears, nor do I perceive them by the thoughts of my own heart or by any combination of my five senses, but in my soul alone, while my outward eyes are open."[3]

She also did it because her truly radical ideas were not all that transparent. Reading Hildegard of Bingen is like looking into a kaleidoscope. Her images shift, move around, disappear and reappear in a rainbow of allusions, alliterations, personifications, and metaphors inside metaphors. A hymn to Ecclesia (a personification of the Church) illustrates her sometimes baffling mix of rhetorical devices:

> O boundless Ecclesia,
> girded with the arms of God
> and arrayed in hyacinth,
> you are the fragrance
> of the wounds of nations,
> the city of Knowledge.
> Amid lofty music
> you have been anointed,
> O glistening gem![4]

Within the verbal flourishes there is order and clear doctrine, and it is powerful material, according to Hildegard scholar Barbara Newman, whose book *Sister of Wisdom: St. Hildegard's Theology of the Feminine* examines both the substance and the wrappings of the saint's teaching and contribution:

Hildegard's is a world in which neither the distinctions of the schoolmen…nor the raptures of the mystics have any place; yet no less than theirs, it is a world…with order, mystery and flaming love. Her universe rings with the most intricate and inviolate harmonies, yet seethes with the strife of relentlessly warring forces.… Soul, body and cosmos interact in patterns as dynamic as they are eccentric. And the living Light irradiates all.[5]

She did it too because she not only studiously abided by the accepted wisdom of the time, which regarded women as weak and subservient, but also made that wisdom her motto and mantra. And then she turned it on its head. She presented herself as a "poor little figure of a woman," beset by illness, lacking in learning, devoid of any right to preach or teach. But was it not an absolute principle of Scripture that God takes the weak things of this world to overcome the strong and the humble things to bring down the proud? Was there not a clear preference in the history of salvation for the lowly, the poor, and the exploited? By reason of this fundamental paradox, Hildegard saw herself justified in presenting to a wide audience those insights that

God mysteriously shared with her, the least of creatures. She taught this paradox and she lived her life according to it.

Finally, she averted any taint of suspicion because she remained orthodox concerning basic Christian discipline and practice. She was a firm advocate of the prerogatives of the pope, the importance of the hierarchy, and the dignity of priests. Hildegard's doctrine was firmly enmeshed in the traditional themes of creation, fall, redemption, and especially, incarnation. Her special affinity for the Old Testament Wisdom (or sapiential) books in no way separated her from other notable teachers of the twelfth century like Bernard of Clairvaux, who regularly used the feminine images in these writings for metaphorical or allegorical purposes. But her use of these images greatly transcended what was normative. "By blending the high traditions of sapiential thought with received ideas about women and weakness," writes Barbara Newman, Hildegard "was able to achieve a distinctive, tense, and highly energized interpretation of the Christian faith."[6]

A MATERNAL GOD

The heavily feminine imagery in Old Testament books like Proverbs and Wisdom has always been both appealing and troublesome for Christian interpreters. For example, Proverbs describes Wisdom as a female existing before the oldest of God's works:

> From everlasting I was firmly set,
>   from the beginning, before the earth came into being.
> The deep was not, when I was born,
>   there were no springs to gush with water.
> Before the mountains were settled,
>   before the hills, I came to birth.[7]

Similarly, the book of Wisdom speaks of Wisdom as

> . . . a breath of the power of God,
>   pure emanation of the glory of the Almighty;
>   hence nothing impure can find a way into her.
>   She is a reflection of the eternal light,

untarnished mirror of God's active power,
image of his goodness.[8]

This kind of exaltation seems to point to a feminine aspect in God's very being. But commentators in the Middle Ages scrupulously followed a strict allegorical reading of such texts, presenting them as imaginative prefigurings of Christ or Mary. One twelfth-century writer, St. Martin of Leon, recognized the problem. An unbeliever, he noted, could well ask the question, "If Christ is the wisdom of God, why is he called a son and not a daughter?" Martin's embarrassed reply was that son is a more "honorable" title than daughter.[9]

Hildegard of Bingen was far more daring in expounding about God in these sapiential terms. Clearly, she was energized by the images in the Wisdom literature and, without contradicting contemporary interpretations, she tried to make explicit and visible what others regarded as inadmissible.

There are three feminine, Godlike personifications that dominate the text of Hildegard's first and best-known book, *Scivias* (an abbreviation of *Scito Vias,* "Know the Ways"). The first is Sapientia, or Lady Wisdom, who appears in a remarkable vision as a quasi-divine presence "both terrible and mild to every creature," the creator and ruler of the world she has made.[10] She is wearing a crown, a golden tunic, and a jeweled stole, but her countenance is too holy to be gazed upon.

Scivias contains a series of illuminated icons depicting Hildegard's visions, produced at her abbey and under her direction. In the center of one is a dominant female figure holding above her head a medallion of Christ, while around the borders are the prophets holding scrolls of their writings. One might naturally assume that the central figure is Mary revealing Jesus, who was foretold of old. She is not Mary, however, but Wisdom; on her garment is written, "I was with him, fashioning all in the beginning."

Writes Nancy Fierro, a current popularizer of Hildegard's message,

Lady Wisdom is the matrix of being, the Creatrix in whom the earth dwells as a child in the mother's womb. She is not a distant prime mover; rather she "looks into the world for people," for she "loves people greatly [and] protects [them] with her own protection. As creatrix-mother she enfolds the universe in her wings and envelops it in her circular odyssey.[11]

As queen, she enjoys the bridal chamber of the most high, since "she is the display of a great beauty gleaming in God... united with him in a most tender embrace, in a dance of blazing love."

A second and similar figure is Caritas, or Lady Love, who says, "I am the most loving consort of the throne of God, and God hides no counsel from me. I keep the royal marriage bed, and all that is God's is mine as well."

In one of her blessings, Hildegard wrote,

> May the Holy Spirit cleanse you from all faults of malice
> and win you the friendship of Love (Caritas)...
> who entered the bridal chamber of all the King's mysteries
> and revealed herself in all her beauty
> in the mirror of the cherubim.

In one passage, Caritas seems almost the alter ego of God the Father as creator: "I am the supreme and fiery force who kindled every living spark, and I breathed forth no deadly thing — yet I permitted all to be. As I circled the whirling sphere with my upper wings... rightly I ordained it.... I quicken all things vitally by an unseen, all sustaining life."

A third feminine manifestation of the divine is Scientia, or the Knowledge of God, who watches over "all people and all things in heaven and on earth, being of such radiance and brightness that, for the measureless splendor that shines in her, you cannot gaze on her face or on the garments she wears." More than the other figures, Scientia represents God's paradoxical awesomeness and simultaneous availability. She is pictured in one place as "shining bright... her eyes blue as jacinth, and her vesture like a mantle of silk. Over her shoulders she wore a bishop's pallium the color of rubies."

A common characteristic in all these feminine images, says Newman, is an emphasis on God's immanence, on God's activity in creation and closeness to creatures, which is revealed preeminently in the incarnation. Male images, in contrast, tend to stress the divine transcendence, God's otherness and distance from the world and from

humanity: "The feminine divine is the revelation of the hidden God
... proposing, revealing, creating, assisting, and alluring.... Through
her the heavens declare the glory of God, the prophets are overshad-
owed by the living Light, and the faithful participate in the Virtues.
Her bearing is regal toward the cosmos, erotic toward God, maternal
toward men and women."[12]

ABBEYS OF EXPRESSIVE FREEDOM

Scholars have studied the background of Hildegard of Bingen, trying
in vain to discover where her exuberant sense of the divine feminine came from; she would, no doubt, have attributed it solely to the
Living Light.

She was born into an aristocratic family of the Rhineland valley in
1098. Her parents, in an exceptionally literal interpretation of the custom of tithing (turning over one-tenth of one's wealth to the Church),
presented her as a tithe — the youngest of their ten children — for
full-time service to the Church at the age of eight. She was sent to live
with a holy hermit woman, Jutta of Sponheim, in a small cottage next
to the monastery of St. Disibod. Here she survived on two meals a
day (served at three in the morning and three in the afternoon), with
her only contacts being Jutta (who provided some minimal education)
and their confessor.

Hildegard, who was plagued with ill health (probably migraine
headaches and asthma) and had experiences of the Living Light from
her earliest years, apparently accepted this austere environment. The
hermitage at St. Disibod attracted so many women that it eventually
became a Benedictine community of nuns with Jutta as the superior.
Sometime during her teenage years, Hildegard took vows as a Benedictine herself and lived a quiet convent life for the next twenty years.
When Jutta died, Hildegard, then thirty-eight, became her successor
as superior. The year was 1136, three years before the Second Lateran
Council would enact a series of reforms, including a ban on usury and
the marriage of clerics.

After assuming authority, Hildegard became convinced she should
no longer remain silent about what she experienced in the Living
Light. She heard a voice that addressed her,

O frail human form from the dust of the earth, ashes from ashes, cry out and proclaim the beginning of undefiled salvation! Let those who see the inner meaning of Scripture, yet do not wish to proclaim or preach it, take instruction, for they are lukewarm and sluggish.... Therefore pour out a fountain of abundance, overflow with mysterious learning, so that those who want you to be despicable on account of Eve's transgression may be overwhelmed by the flood of your profusion.[13]

And so she did, though she continually struggled with doubts about her worthiness and with regular bouts of illness. Her writings and correspondence brought fame to the abbey as well as a swarm of new novices. In 1150, after a titanic tussle with the abbot at St. Disibod, who wanted to keep her there, Hildegard moved on, establishing a new foundation at Rupertsberg, near Bingen. She brought with her some fifty nuns. As the population of that abbey swelled too, she founded in 1165 a sister house in Eibingen, some eight miles away.

At both these locales, Hildegard attempted to recognize on a day-to-day basis the exalted sense of the feminine she had seen in her visions. Both convents were built according to her instructions, with large workshops and rooms that had the unheard-of luxury of piped-in water. The nuns were provided opportunity to develop their spiritual, intellectual, and artistic talents. They copied and illustrated manuscripts, wove, learned to sing and to play musical instruments, and heard lectures on theology. The nuns also made use of Hildegard's health tips, including warm baths and regular exercise. She promoted the drinking of beer because, she said, it was better than the local water and gave the nuns "rosy cheeks."

Nancy Fierro describes the "expressive freedom" that came to be associated with the Bingen and Eibingen abbeys:

These women celebrated holy days by wearing white veils, tiaras with gems, and putting rings on their fingers. When another Rhineland abbess criticized Hildegard for the fancy clothing her nuns wore, she responded that it was women's place to "flash and radiate" Divine beauty. She also reminded the abbess that the monastic virgin had a right to adorn herself beyond the secular matron because it was done out of love for the heavenly bridegroom.[14]

In all this she seemed determined to avoid the contradictions lurking behind much medieval spirituality. Writers might well praise the abstract divine feminine in the Bible's Wisdom literature, but would regard women in reality in quite another way — in keeping with the blatant misogynist passages in those very same Wisdom books, such as Ecclesiasticus: "The beauty of a woman is a snare and a delusion," "the daughter is a burden to her father," and "from a woman came the beginning of sin, and by her we all die."[15]

MAN "CREATED FOR WOMAN"

Hildegard's writings on women were deeply rooted in her insights on the feminine in God. She was especially fascinated with a woman's role in the incarnation and saw it as a kind of template for the call of all women to bring God into the world. And since Jesus was formed, as it were, in the image of Mary (with no male involvement), it seemed to Hildegard that woman is a far more appropriate model than man for redeemed human nature. She did not carry this idea to its logical conclusion, concerning who would therefore be the most appropriate presider at the Eucharist, nor did she put these ideas in overt, unambiguous language. Such candor would surely have aroused great alarm in her era. The *Decretum,* an early expression of Church law published only two years after she became abbess, declared, "The image of God is in man in such a way that there is only one Lord... having the power of God as God's vicar... and thus woman is not made in God's image."[16] Even the most liberal theologian of Hildegard's time, Peter Abelard, held that man enjoys a "more express likeness" to God because he excels "in the godly attributes of power, wisdom, and love."[17]

Yet, on this issue of the relative dignity of male and female, Hildegard was dangerously direct, going so far as to contradict St. Paul's statement in First Corinthians 11:8–9: "For man did not come from woman; no, woman came from man; and man was not created for the sake of woman, but woman was created for the sake of man."

It may be true, Hildegard said, that woman was created for man, but it is equally true "that man was created for woman. For [if] she is from man, so too man is from her, lest one be sundered from the other in the unity of procreation. For in one activity they perform one act, just as the air and the wind work together." Besides, she pointed out, while man may have "greater strength than woman, yet woman is a fountain of wisdom and a wellspring of deep joy," which man draws on.[18]

Hildegard went to special lengths to relieve Eve of the enormous guilt laid upon her by medieval interpreters — and by extension on all the daughters of Eve. No, she insisted, Satan did not approach the woman first because she was intellectually and morally inferior to her husband, as Augustine taught; he approached Eve out of envy for her potential for motherhood. She may have been vulnerable, admitted Hildegard, because women are more open and trusting by nature, but the true villain in Paradise was the devil, who poured his poison on the fruit. When Adam and Eve ate of it equally, they both caught the devil's disease.

She struggled with the Augustinian idea that sexual pleasure is both a penalty for sin and somehow sinful in itself, eventually coming to the conclusion that the pleasure is not sinful. Nevertheless, she concurred that women's menstruation is a penalty, but then approached it in a decidedly unorthodox way. She heard God saying, "I do not disdain this time of suffering in woman, for I gave it to Eve when she conceived sin in the taste of the fruit. So a woman during her period should be treated with the great medicine of mercy."[19] No such consideration should be given, she added, to those who deliberately shed blood in warfare.

PLACED UNDER INTERDICT!

At no time during the bulk of her public career was Hildegard reprimanded by clerics or theologians for her distinctively radical ideas. At one point her writings were examined by representatives of Pope Eugenius III and found acceptable. She was, after all, a seer. The implications of her teachings could be neither grasped easily nor, in the view of Church authorities, need they be taken too seriously. That equanimity would be instantly dissipated when Hildegard — apparently for the first time in her life — openly defied legitimate Church authority. The year was 1178, and she was eighty years old.

A young man who had been excommunicated for his alleged involvement in revolutionary activity died, and Hildegard gave permission for him to be buried in the cemetery at the Rupertsberg abbey. In the absence of the bishop of Mainz, who had jurisdiction over the abbey, the canons at the cathedral ordered Hildegard to exhume the body from consecrated ground. She protested that she had it on the highest authority that the sins of the young man had been absolved, and she even traveled to Mainz to make her case.

The canons rejected her argument and authorized local civil authorities to go to the cemetery and dig up the offending body. The evening before their arrival, Hildegard, vested in her formal attire as abbess and with her staff in hand, went to the grave and solemnly blessed it. She then quietly removed cemetery markers and gravestones, so the plot of the man could not be identified.

The irate canons placed the abbey under interdict, which meant that Mass and the sacraments could not be celebrated there, nor could the nuns sing the divine office. The ban on music was especially painful to Hildegard, and she wrote strong words to the canons and still-absent bishop, reminding them that those who silence God's praises in this life will most assuredly be relegated in the afterlife to "the place of no music." The problem dragged on for many months, until the interdict was finally lifted in March of 1179. Hildegard died peacefully six months later.

Veneration of the abbess began almost immediately, with a stream of pilgrims arriving at Bingen, seeking her intercession for cures and other favors. The throng grew so large that the nuns at the abbey, according to legend, eventually asked the bishop to order Hildegard under obedience to cease working miracles. It is not recorded whether he did so, but the pilgrim crowds finally thinned out in the thirteenth century. The process of her beatification, begun some sixty years after her death, was never completed in Rome, and the reasons are not clear. Nevertheless, her local cult remained strong in the Rhineland area. In 1940 the Vatican officially recognized her sanctity as established by long-term popular acclamation and provided a feast day for her in the liturgy (September 17).

A SEMINAL FIGURE

It cannot be claimed that Hildegard of Bingen's views have been thoroughly vindicated in the modern Church. Problems associated with gender, inclusive language, and the proper role of women in liturgy and ministry remain pervasive and neuralgic. Still, so much has changed that a host of twelfth-century assumptions about God, women, and scriptural interpretation have simply passed away. And she is a mighty, seminal figure in the change.

An exclusively male concept of God is no longer possible, according to the *Catechism of the Catholic Church:* "In no way is God in man's image. He is neither man nor woman. God is pure spirit in which there is no place for the differences between the sexes. But the respective perfections of man and woman reflect something of the infinite perfection of God: those of a mother and those of a father and husband."[20]

References to these feminine reflections of God appear now and again at the highest levels of Church authority. Speaking to a crowd at St. Peter's square in 1978, Pope John Paul I said, "We are the objects of undying love on the part of God.... God is our father; even more God is our mother. God does not want to hurt us, but only to do good for us.... If children are ill they have additional claim to be loved by their mother. And we too, if by chance we are sick with badness and are on the wrong track, have yet another claim to be loved by the Lord."[21] In his 1992 encyclical *Dives in misericordia,* Pope John Paul II noted that the Hebrew term *rachamim* (applied to God in the Old Testament) connotes the bond of love between mother and child. "Of this love one can say that it is completely gratuitous, unmerited," he wrote. "It [*rachamim*] is, as it were, a feminine variation" of masculine terms for God's faithfulness and concern.[22]

No Catholic theologian today would question the fundamental equality of man and woman. Although the Second Vatican Council gave scant attention to women (six specific references to women in all the documents compared to 112 to priests), it did take notice of this equality in *Gaudium et Spes:* "Women claim for themselves an equity with men before the law and in fact.... Now for the first time in human history, all people are convinced that the benefits of culture ought to be and actually can be extended to everyone."[23]

The literal interpretation of Scripture at times used to support misogynist views has been effectively replaced by a far more nuanced
approach. In a passage that Hildegard would surely have applauded,
Vatican II declared in *Dei Verbum,* "For there is a growth in the understanding of the realities and the words which have been handed down.
This happens through the contemplation and study made by believers who treasure these things in their hearts, through the intimate
understanding of spiritual things they experience."[24]

In the last forty years of the twentieth century, the Church wit-
nessed a flood of books, articles, conferences, and courses on Christian
feminism. Consistently recognized in this effort is the very early contribution of Hildegard of Bingen, a woman of her time, yet well
ahead of her time in the breadth of her perspective. Pope John Paul II
called her "a light to her people and her time [who] shines out more
brightly today."[25]

Says Nancy Fierro:

> There is a thirst for the kind of balanced and colorful spirituality
> that she provides. To a world torn by ... violence ... she brings her
> fresh view of a regenerative, cooperative universe alive with Di-
> vine Wisdom and Love.... For women in particular, Hildegard
> brings hope by showing us a vision of the Divine that affirms us
> as women — our bodies, our minds, our hearts and our powers.[26]

NINE

YVES CONGAR

A Passion for Unity

The career of the French Dominican theologian Yves-Marie Congar was marked over a twenty-year period by a series of mystifying milestones:

- June 1937: Congar, then a young professor of theology, is denied permission to attend, as an observer, an ecumenical conference in England.

- April 1939: Congar is summoned to Paris by the Dominican master general and informed that Rome has "very serious difficulties" with his book *Divided Christendom (Chretiens Desunis* in the original French edition), published two years before. The nature of the difficulties is not made clear.

- May 1942: During his five years as a prisoner of war in a German camp in Silesia, he learns that the school where he taught has been upbraided by Rome and a book about its methods suppressed.

- December 1947: Congar's superiors reject his request to write an article on the Catholic Church's official position on ecumenism.

- June 1948: He is informed that Rome has denied his request to be an observer at the founding meeting of the World Council of Churches; nor will anyone else be permitted to observe.

- August 1948: Congar submits a revised, second edition of his book to the Dominican censors but hears nothing for two years. He is then told that alterations will be required but is not made aware of what must be changed. No second edition is ever published.

- February 1952: The Holy Office forbids a second edition of Congar's next book, *True and False Reform* (*Vrai et Fausse Reforme dans l'Eglise* in French), and bars translation of the work into any foreign language. In addition, he is told that all his writings hereafter must be sent directly to Rome for approval prior to publication.

- February 1954: Congar is called to Paris and notified that he and several associates by order of the Holy Office are removed from their teaching posts and required (at least temporarily) to leave France.

- September 1954: He returns from Jerusalem, where, during his exile, he has written yet another book (it will go through seven censors with publication delayed for four years). He is then ordered to Rome for three months.

- February 1955: He is again exiled, this time to England, where he is virtually under house arrest and forbidden to have any contact with Protestants.

- December 1955: Congar is assigned to a monastery in Strasbourg, France; here he has a bit more freedom during the next four years, though his actions and activities remain under a cloud.

Three questions immediately suggest themselves in light of this litany of misery. What did the man do to merit such punishment? Why did he stay at his task and continue to irritate those in authority for such a length of time? And finally, how did Yves Congar become one of the best-known, most admired, and highly honored theologians of the twentieth century — even a member of the Sacred College of Cardinals in his last year?

RESTLESS ACTIVIST

The answer to the first question is relatively simple. Congar, by his own admission, was "nothing but a nuisance" to his superiors.[1] He

became, by choice, a tireless ambassador of ecumenism without port-
folio at a time when Rome's attitude toward interchurch relations was
at best ambiguous and at worst hostile. No steps of cooperation with
non-Catholics were to be taken except at the highest levels of authority
and only with the greatest caution. Yet here was this unflappable little
Frenchman, writing books and arranging meetings and conferences
with Protestant and Orthodox churchmen, constantly pushing at the
limits. He became, in the view of Rome, a loose cannon, a troublemaker, an ignorer of protocol, and a dissenter from accepted discipline
and doctrine.

Indeed, the traditional doctrine of the Church with regard to non-
Catholic Christians had been exceptionally harsh. The Council of
Florence in the fifteenth century, for example, declared, "All who
are outside the Catholic Church, not only pagans but also Jews,
heretics and schismatics, cannot partake of eternal life, but are doomed
to the eternal fire of hell."[2] In more modern times, gradual signs
of accommodation appeared. Pope Leo XIII in the late nineteenth
century referred in his writing to "dissidents" and "separated ones"
rather than "heretics" and "schismatics." Pope Pius XI in the 1920s
displayed a special fondness for Orthodox Christians and even admitted that both East and West shared blame for the major division in
Catholicism.

Still, the sole solution to division remained the same as ever: those
in error must renounce their error and return to the one, true fold.
Meanwhile, the 1917 Code of Canon Law stated, "It is not licit for
the faithful to assist in any way, that is, to take part in the liturgies
of non-Catholics."[3] And, despite his warm feelings, Pius XI forbade
Catholics to attend any meetings or conventions "at which all without
distinction are invited to join the discussion, both infidels of every
kind, and Christians, even those who have unhappily fallen away from
Christ or with obstinacy and pertinacity deny His divine nature and
mission.... The Apostolic See has never allowed Catholics to attend
meetings of non-Catholics."[4]

Pius was here reacting defensively to a significant development
occurring in worldwide Protestantism: the birth of the Ecumenical
Movement. It began in 1910 with the formation in Scotland of the
International Missionary Council. Then in 1925 came the Life and

Work Movement founded in Sweden, which emphasized the commonalities of the various denominations; its motto was "Service unites but doctrine divides." In 1927 yet another initiative, the Faith and Order Movement, launched in Switzerland, recognized that doctrine too had to be addressed before union was possible.

In the 1930s the Catholic Church watched from a distance with queasy apprehension as the three ventures began to coalesce toward what would eventually become one megamovement, the National Council of Churches. There were elements of both attraction and repulsion in what these non-Catholics were attempting. Hadn't Jesus prayed that all his followers be one? Hadn't the Church too prayed for that from the beginning? But as the Church had always said, unity must be on Catholic terms — unconditional surrender or nothing. Besides, there were disturbing elements of doctrinal relativism in this Protestant-based ecumenism. So Rome chose to move sometimes forward, sometimes backward on the issue: a bit of encouragement to the separated brethren here, a warning against collaboration with outsiders there.

Congar did not follow the script. His enthusiasm was such that he heard the encouragment as the voice of the Holy Spirit and the warning as a well-intentioned expression of temporary prudence. On his own initiative at the age of thirty-two he wrote *Divided Christendom,* the first of some forty volumes of theology and reflection he would author in his lifetime. By today's measure, the tone of the book was anything but radical; he went to extremes in his defense of Roman Catholicism and in his criticism of many Protestant and Orthodox positions. The first edition of the book easily passed the censors' scrutiny. But it proved to have more impact than a book like this might be expected to have; it got people thinking, talking, and then writing about ecumenism in a new way. Vatican officials read the book carefully and began to worry. Prior to *Divided Christendom,* modern Catholic theology was willing to recognize the goodwill and basic Christianity of individual Protestant, Anglican, and especially, Orthodox Christians. It was often said that such persons were somehow connected to the one, true Church through an "implicit *votum*" — a "desire" to be Catholic that they were not aware of. However, theology was not prepared to agree that the non-Catholic church bodies to which they belonged had an essential respectability *as churches* or any objective justification to exist in their own right.

Congar was among the first to consider in a systematic way how and why these bodies should be viewed more positively:

> If schisms have endured, if Lutheranism for example, can show four hundred years of existence and fifty millions of adherents, if other schisms have equally lasted and grown and have produced many remarkable lives consecrated to God, this must be due not to what they deny and reject, but to what they affirm and assert. When we try to understand why thousands of truly religious souls have a deep and inward attachment to the erroneous forms of Christianity they were born in and why they have a deep and inward repugnance to the Catholic Church, we find that they are attached to certain values which they regard as essential to Christianity and as lost or distorted in the Catholic Church, such things as Christian liberty, the primacy of interior faith over outward practice, the sense of mystery and of the free initiative of God, nay even genuine loyalty and true evangelical simplicity of life.[5]

Such churches, he explained, contain *vestigia* (manifestations) of true Christianity and must be respected in a certain sense as holy: "In this sense it may be said that Lutheranism and Calvinism, regarded in the light of their original religious inspiration, ... are capable of integration with the Church, or rather that they may be found within its orbit as units in the whole, though not as Lutheranism or Calvinism."[6]

Congar carefully followed up these insights with a lengthy justification for the Church's failure to become involved in non-Catholic efforts at unity: the movement is only in its beginning stages; the Church might lose its uniqueness if it participated in discussions as an equal; public discussions of theology might distort or compromise the Church's message.

CERTAIN FAULTS IN CATHOLICISM

Despite these qualifications, which, Congar thought, indicated the book's basically orthodox orientation, Rome was not pleased — especially when some theologians of note began to elaborate on these ideas. Inspired by *Divided Christendom,* Jacques Maritain wrote on the "supernaturally created personality" of the Church present in an invisible way in non-Catholic communities. And Dominican theologian Christophe Dumont suggested that Protestant churches really have "the whole" of Christianity, though they express it only partially and deficiently.

Congar's book *True and False Reform,* published in 1950, also aroused concern somewhat belatedly. As in the previous work, Congar presented his ideas calmly, without any suggestion of troubling the waters. Church reform, he said, "is not a matter of reforming abuses, for there virtually are none. It is a question of revising structures. That goes beyond a simple reminder of what the canons require. It demands a climbing up higher towards the sources."

Yet, he went on, "certain historico-cultural faults" can be observed in the institutional structures. In particular, he said, the priestly office can become bound up to "devotional expressions characteristic of a given time" and the magisterium can be tied too closely to "particular forms of authority," so that the holy and apostolic mission is "hindered by human limitations." Congar wrote of two great temptations confronting the Church in every age: "Pharisaism," that is, absolutizing religious rules and regulations rather than serving the spiritual and pastoral needs of the people; and "the temptation of the Synagogue," that is, freezing tradition in such a way that it cannot develop beyond what was understood in the past. What the Church must do, he insisted, is harmonize itself more generously with the style of a new society — "a society she [the Church] is called to baptize as she has baptized others in the past."[7]

The book passed censorship in the first edition, only to be found dangerously misleading on further consideration by Vatican authorities. There was one obvious reason. *True and False Reform* was published almost simultaneously with the release of Pius XII's encyclical *Humani generis.* In it the pope railed against those who would recklessly accommodate Church doctrine to modern times. "Some are presumptive enough," he said, "to question seriously whether theology...should not only be perfected, but also completely reformed, in order to promote the more efficacious prorogation of the kingdom of Christ." Twice in the text Pius spoke against a false and imprudent "irenicism" — that is, an attitude of peaceful acceptance of erroneous opinions. "There are many," he said, "who, deploring disagreement . . . and intellectual confusion, through an imprudent zeal for souls, are urged . . . to do away with the barrier that divides good and honest men; these advocate an irenicism, according to which . . . they aim not only at joining forces to repel the attacks of atheism, but also at reconciling things opposed to one another in the field of dogma."[8]

Pius here not only was referring to unapproved ecumenical effort, but also was confronting in particular an entire coterie of avant garde French theologians who were striving in various ways at the time to bring the Church into closer contact with the modern, increasingly unbelieving world. The thrust was called the *Nouvelle Théologie* (New Theology), and its French practitioners included, besides Congar, Henri de Lubac, Emmanuel Mounier, Jean Daniélou, Congar's mentor and friend Marie Dominique Chenu, and a dozen or more others. There had been complaints for some time that this talk of accommodation was Modernism in disguise. *Humani generis* was meant to be taken seriously, as more than a shot across the bow.

Ironically, the phenomenon that resulted in Congar's exile in 1954 — and similar disciplinary action against others — was not ecumenism as such. It was the Worker-Priest Movement, an expression of the New Theology (but one with which Congar was only tangentially involved). Begun in the early 1940s in reaction to worker alienation from the Church, the movement eventually involved some one hundred priests who worked in French factories and on the docks and lived just like their lay coworkers. The intention was to somehow insert the Church's message of creation and redemption directly into the industrial world. Chenu, who developed the intellectual rationale, declared, "The proletarian masses are destined to produce in their own being this will and this hope [for human community]. They will redeem the world."[9] But the experiment had not gone as well as hoped. The worker-priests stirred criticism among conservative Catholics, other priests, and some bishops. That priests should be involved in union organizing, marching in protests, and consorting with Communists aroused alarm and scandal. The worker-priests, for their part, became outspokenly militant; they accused the institutional Church of abandoning the working class and decried Catholicism's medieval appearance and individualistic morality.

The climax came in 1953 when France's three most prominent cardinals were called to Rome and ordered to curb the movement. In early 1954 worker-priests were told to return to their rectories, give up all union activity, and limit themselves to no more than three hours of worldly work a day. Said the archbishop of Lille, "To be a priest and to be a worker are two functions, two different states of life, and it is not possible to unite them in the same person without altering the notion of priesthood."[10] About one-third of the worker-priests complied with the orders, while the rest chose to remain on their jobs despite sanctions.

Congar had given retreats for some of these worker-priests and had publicly called their ministry an important opening up of the Church to the world. However, he had not been, like Chenu, an active participant in the movement. Nevertheless, the crackdown was deemed by the Vatican as an appropriate time to scatter and silence many associated with the New Theology. Congar was shipped off to Jerusalem, to Rome, to England, to Austria. Chenu, de Lubac, Daniélou, and others tarred with the same brush were also disciplined.

A SERIES OF DENUNCIATIONS

In his later years Congar explained in some detail why he pressed forward on ecumenical issues for so long when it was perfectly clear that higher Church authority did not appreciate his efforts: he fervently believed he had a vocation to ecumenism. It came to him, he said, as he was preparing for his ordination to the priesthood in 1930: "It was while meditating upon the seventeenth chapter of St. John's Gospel [Jesus' prayer that all may be one] that I clearly recognized my vocation to work for the unity of all who believe in Jesus Christ. Ever since the days immediately following my ordination, I have often repeated that prayer."[11]

He was soon assigned to teach theology at Le Saulchoir, a Dominican house of studies in Belgium, and there he came under the charismatic influence of Chenu, who was afire with the intellectual and theological revival in France during the 1920s and early 1930s. Great thinkers like Etienne Gilson, Gabriel Marcel, Jacques Maritain, Pierre Maury, and Nicholas Berdyaev were in their prime. Between classes and conferences at Le Saulchoir, Congar spent his time in Paris soaking in the inspiration of such men. "A great enterprise was afoot to open up the Catholic ghetto wide upon the world," he said.[12]

He made contact with Orthodox and Protestant leaders, establishing friendships with many. While on a trip to Germany, he first realized that "there were depths in Luther which demanded investigation and understanding." He met the outstanding Protestant theologian Karl Barth and organized a Catholic symposium on the man's work when Barth came to Paris. Congar also visited frequently the Benedictine monastery at Amay, which housed monks of both the Eastern and Western rites, and he established a close relationship with the monastery's founder, Dom Lambert Beauduin, an early pioneer in ecumenism. He also came to know Abbé Paul Couturier, who was vigorously promoting the celebration of the Christian Unity Octave in France. Congar was invited in 1936 to preach during the eight days of the octave at historic Sacred Heart Church in Paris, and the material of these talks he transformed the following year into *Chretiens Desunis*. The Unity Octave, with its prayers and hymns for full reunion, became a spiritual highpoint in his life. Except for his years in the prison camp, he preached somewhere during the octave every year from 1936 until his health declined in the 1980s. He later said,

> It very soon occurred to me that ecumenism...presupposes a movement of conversion and reform co-extensive with the whole life of all communions. It seemed to me also that each individual's ecumenical task lay in the first place at home among his own people. Our business was to rotate the Catholic Church through a few degrees on its own axis in the direction of convergence towards others and a possible unanimity with them....For this reason I spread myself to a certain extent. I thought it my duty to do so and I do not regret it.[13]

But by 1937 the young priest's commitment to these activities had begun to attract attention in Rome. When Congar routinely requested permission to attend a conference in Oxford, England, an ecumenical event he had helped to organize, permission was denied. The ruling, he was told, came from Msgr. Eugenio Pacelli, Vatican secretary of state and the future Pope Pius XII.

Congar's ecumenical interests led naturally to an interest in Catholic Church reform. "To some extent," he wrote, "we are to blame for unbelief, and this seemed to me to arise from the fact that the Church shows...a face which belies rather than expresses her true nature.... The real response would be a renewal of our presentation of the Church and above all...a renewal of our own view of the Church transcending the juridical idea of her which has been dominant for so long."[14]

In 1939 Congar was drafted into the French army and served as a chaplain before being captured by the Germans. And this five-year internment, mostly in the repressive Colditz fortress, temporarily deflated his ecumenical enthusiasm. "The dominant impression [among Protestant and Orthodox Christians whom he rubbed shoulders with in prison] is one of distrust and repulsion with regard to Rome," he said. It was during this time that a book by Chenu, *Le Saulchoir: A School of Theology,* was banned by Rome, and Chenu himself was censured. The school (and the book's) open-to-the-world approach was found to be too open, and Congar believed that he escaped personal censure at the time only because he was incarcerated.

When freed in 1945, he was delighted to learn that the Vatican appeared to be taking a small step forward on ecumenism. A Dutch abbot, Jan Willebrands, told him that several members of the Roman Curia, including Cardinal Augustin Bea, had given permission for the formation of a Catholic Council for Ecumenical Questions. Willebrands wanted Congar to become involved, and asked him to put together a series of reports on Catholic ecumenical perspectives for consideration by those organizing the foundational assembly of the World Council of Churches, to be held in Geneva in August of 1948. Congar, of course, complied, since he personally knew many of the Protestant and Orthodox leaders involved, including the man who would become the World Council's first president, W. A. Visser 't Hooft.

Early in 1948 World Council organizers asked Congar to attend as a private observer the founding assembly and to suggest ten other

Catholics who might like to observe the proceedings. Delighted, Congar sought authorization from the archbishop of Paris, who referred him to the archbishop of Utrecht, who said he believed that Rome would permit only four Catholics to attend and that he, the archbishop, had already chosen the fortunate four. While Congar attempted in vain to cut through the red tape, notice came from the Holy Office that neither he nor any other Catholic could expect authorization to attend. Congar then organized and preached at a special Mass in Paris in August to commemorate the launch of the World Council. "I thought it desirable that there should be a manifestation of sympathy and prayer on the part of Catholics during the Amsterdam Assembly," he said. "I showed that the 'No' said to the ecumenical movement and the Amsterdam Assembly was not all that the Church had to say to them and that there were also more positive aspects of our attitude."

Yet, he admitted, the observer incident "was very painful to me and was a turning point in my ecumenical activities. I then realized something which I already suspected: I was simply not made for any sort of negotiation, whatever it might be."

After that, his problems with authority only escalated. Later he recalled, "From the beginning of 1947 to the end of 1956 I knew nothing from that quarter [the Vatican] but an uninterrupted series of denunciations, warnings, restrictive or discriminatory measures, and mistrustful interventions."[15] He could not get his books reviewed by censors, and even when they did examine them, he was required to make countless alterations. Complaints about his collaboration with "heretics and schismatics" were constantly passed on to him. His every move required approval by his Dominican superiors, and approval was often not forthcoming. When exile came in 1954, Congar accepted the verdict without protest and began to write about a new subject, the role of the laity in the Church, though he had no assurance that any of it would ever be published. In 1963 he wrote about his endurance in those years:

> Anyone who is acquainted with me knows that I am impatient
> in little things. I am incapable of waiting for a bus. I believe,
> however, that in big things I am patient in an active way.... This

is something quite different from merely marking time. It is a quality of mind, or better of the heart, which is rooted in the profound existential conviction, firstly that God is in charge and accomplishes his gracious design through us, and secondly that, in all great things, delay is necessary for their maturation.[16]

"THE EXPERTS TO WHOM WE LISTEN"

The rehabilitation of Yves Congar from disgraced troublemaker to Catholic luminary occurred quickly with the election of Pope John XXIII in 1958. The overshadowing cloud evaporated, as it did for others associated with the New Theology like Chenu, de Lubac, and Daniélou. Quietly, Congar pursued again his ecumenical vocation and discovered that his books easily passed censorship. Ecumenism, Church reform, and lay involvement had become topics of universal interest almost overnight.

In 1960 Pope John, preparing for the Second Vatican Council, appointed Cardinal Augustin Bea as first president of the Secretariat for Church Unity. Bea chose Jan Willebrands as secretary of the new body, and Willebrands immediately sought out his old associate Yves Congar, who, he noted, probably knew more about Catholic ecumenism than any living human. So it happened that Congar attended all the council sessions as a *peritus* (expert), advising cardinals, bishops, and other theologians regarding the documents that would seek to open the Church to the world. His work was almost entirely behind the scenes, though there was applause at one general session of the council when Cardinal Michele Pellegrino said, referring to Congar and Chenu, "There are theologians who once had sanctions against them and were even exiled, and who now are the experts to whom we listen."[17]

Congar's expertise was sought in developing the Constitutions on the Church, the Laity, Revelation, and the Church in the World. And he was especially active in advising Bea and Willebrands during the testy battle over the wording of the Decree on Ecumenism. (True to his word, he stayed clear of the negotiations.) In its final form that document sums up one of the main themes of Congar's entire life:

- Today in many parts of the world, under the inspiring grace of the Holy Spirit, multiple efforts are being expended...to attain that fullness of unity which Jesus Christ desires. This sacred Synod therefore exhorts all the Catholic faithful to recognize the signs of the times and to participate skillfully in the works of ecumenism.

- The brethren divided from us also carry out many of the sacred actions of the Christian religion. Undoubtedly...these actions can truly engender a life of grace, and can be rightly described as capable of providing access to the community of salvation.

- The Catholic Church accepts them with respect and affection as brothers. For men who believe in Christ and have been properly baptized are brought into a certain, though imperfect, communion with the Catholic Church.

- It follows that these separated Churches and Communities... have by no means been deprived of significance and importance in the mystery of salvation. For the Spirit of Christ has not refrained from using them as means of salvation.

- Christ summons the Church, as she goes her pilgrim way, to that continual reformation of which she always has need, insofar as she is an institution of men here on earth. Therefore, if the influence of events or of the times has led to deficiencies in conduct, in Church discipline, or even in the formulation of doctrine...these should be appropriately rectified at the proper moment.[18]

Following the council, Pope Paul VI appointed Congar a member of the Catholic-Lutheran dialogue and of the newly founded Pontifical International Theological Commission. In 1966 he was among the pope's invitees to a special congress in Rome celebrating the theology of Vatican II. He was publicly honored there with others who had experienced hard times: Karl Rahner, Edward Schillebeeckx, and John Courtney Murray. The ecumenical character of the event was underscored by the arrival of the old patriarch of Protestant theology, Karl Barth, who tottered down the aisle with his equally frail wife amidst great applause.

Congar's literary output scarcely slackened during the thirty years following the council, but he was increasingly enfeebled by a neurological disorder that gradually left him unable to walk. He wrote books on spirituality, the Holy Spirit, Mary, Martin Luther, St. Augustine, St. Thomas Aquinas, the challenges of the modern world, and, of course, ecumenism — amassing more than fifteen hundred book and article entries in the Vatican Library catalog.

In 1985 Pope John Paul II invited Congar, then eighty-one, to attend in Rome a special synod of bishops called to reevaluate Vatican II, but he was living in a nursing home by that time and unable to attend. As late as 1989, however, he was still writing and giving interviews. In 1994, just six months before Congar's death, John Paul conferred upon him the red hat of cardinal.

In his latter days Congar reflected on the perspective and sense of balance that sustained him throughout his trials:

> The Church has been a...peaceable place for my faith and my prayer. And why not?...Assuredly, there is a lot of narrow mindedness and immaturity, many botched works in the Church. We see too in many spheres how unprepared the Church is to offer answers to the true questions posed by men. But all that, as heavy a burden as it may be for us to bear, is of no importance when it is balanced against what I can find and actually do find in the Church. The Church has been, and is, the hearth of my soul; the mother of my spiritual being. She offers me the possibility of living with the saints: and when did she ever prevent me from living a Christian life?[19]

TEN

CREATIVE DIFFERENCES

This chapter considers in more abbreviated form five Church figures whose dissent, real or imputed, served the long-term good of the Christian people at very different times and under different circumstances.

Thomas Aquinas

THEODORE: ONE PERSON, TWO NATURES

The case of Theodore of Mopsuestia ranks among the strangest miscarriages of justice in Church history. Declared a teacher of heresy and excommunicated more than a century after his death, he has since been largely vindicated for his work in formulating orthodox doctrine.

He was an especially active theologian in the fifth century, when the age of the martyrs had ended, Christianity had been established as the official doctrine of the Roman Empire, and believers had the luxury of pondering the intellectual implications of their faith in Jesus Christ.

What did it mean to say that God became a human being? Isn't God immutable and unchangeable? And what did it mean to say that the Word became flesh? Was Jesus a real human or only an apparent one? Such questions exercised the minds of both scholars and ordinary citizens of the fifth century. It was said that one could not go into a barbershop in Alexandria or Antioch, the two great centers of theological thought, without getting involved in a discussion or argument about the true nature of Christ. Christians recognized that their faith was wrapped in mystery, but they felt a great need to study the wholly holy through reason and analogy in hopes of making the mystery more approachable.

In Alexandria the emphasis was on Christ's divinity. He was, as the Council of Nicea said in 325, "God from God" and "*one in being* with the Father." In Antioch the focus centered on his humanity. The "Word was made *flesh*...and was *like us* in all things except sin." Either position could easily lead to gross exaggeration, and the times were rife with unpronounceable theories like Apollinarianism and Eutychianism.

No one tried harder to reconcile the divergent aspects of the divinity-humanity question than Theodore, the bishop of Mopsuestia from 392 to 428. Mopsuestia, located in what is now southern Turkey, was then a growing center of Christianity, and Theodore wanted to make the faith as intelligible as possible to his catechumens. It was in this context, over a period of many years, that he expounded more clearly than others before him the concept that in Christ there are two natures (or principles of operation), one divine and one human, subsisting in the one person, Jesus, who is the Word, the Son of God.

Theodore, who leaned toward the Antioch school, opposed what he saw as an excessive Alexandrian emphasis on divinity. He firmly believed that humans were saved through Christ's humanity and that it is Christ as human who serves as mediator between God and the human race. He wrote voluminously on this subject, both in popular form for ordinary citizens and in dense theology for the experts. His opponent during most of his active years was Cyril, bishop of Alexandria; the two engaged in a lively debate, much of which has been preserved.

As a proponent of Christ's humanity, Theodore was not especially fond of expressions like "Mary is the mother of God" or "For us God died on the cross." But he recognized that what was known as the "communication of idioms" allowed a certain attribution of divine characteristics to the human Christ and human characteristics to the incarnate divine Word. Yet, he feared that such expressions, unless properly understood, could elevate the figure of Christ to such heights that the humanity would be lost. (This is exactly what the Apollinarists, and later the Monophysites, did.)

Wrote Theodore, "He became man.... And it was not through a simple providence that he lowered himself, nor was it through the gift of powerful help [to an ordinary human], as he has done so often and still does. Rather did he take our very nature; he clothed himself with it and dwelt in it so as to make it perfect through sufferings; and he united himself with it."[1]

The two natures, divine and human, were joined in what Theodore called a *prosopon*—which is roughly equivalent to our word "person." There was, of course, a possibility of confusion here. Did the union of the natures, according to Theodore, create a new person who did not exist before, and was this *prosopon* that of the Word, the Son of God? On this subject much debate occurred, but scholars have generally agreed with Aloys Grillmeier that "the authentic Theodore always speaks only of one *prosopon* in two natures."[2] Or as Theodore himself wrote, "The Logos [Word] united ... [the human nature] as a whole to himself and made him to share with him [the Word] in all the dignity which he who indwells, being Son [of God] by nature, participates."[3]

Theodore died in peace in the year 428, and that's when the real trouble started. One of Theodore's early students, Nestorius, bishop of Constantinople, got into deep trouble with Cyril of Alexandria by publicly criticizing the use of expressions such as "God died on the cross." Nor were his criticisms well received by ordinary believers whose piety was offended. Instead of trying to explain what he really meant, Nestorius only developed his ideas further, so that he seemed to be teaching that in Christ there were not only two natures but two persons (or maybe three persons when the other two merged into a new composite person in Christ). Greatly complicated by political and personal intrigues, the battle between Nestorius and Cyril escalated until Cyril managed to have Nestorius condemned as a heretic at the Council of Ephesus in 431.[4] In the years that followed, those who exaggerated Christ's divinity evolved into what became known as "Monophysites" (Greek for "holders of one nature"). They concentrated entirely on Christ's divine nature and his divine person, thus submerging (or destroying) his humanity. At the Council of Chalcedon, in 451, this Monophysite position was condemned, and the assembled bishops proclaimed in precise terms what Theodore had been getting at in his lifetime:

We confess one and the same Son, who is our Lord Jesus Christ, and we all agree in teaching that this very same Son is complete in his deity and complete...in his humanity, truly God and truly a human being.... The character of each nature is preserved and comes together in one person...not divided or torn into two persons but one and the same Son and only begotten God.[5]

Chalcedon would seem to have had the last word. But wait! The Monophysites would not yield so easily. They insisted that they had been misunderstood, and created great problems in the Church for almost a century as they propagated their interpretation as superior to the doctrine of Chalcedon. They were not successful, but they still sought to eke out a concession. If they could not have their old heresy endorsed, at least they hoped to strike a blow at the long-dead theologian whose insights prepared the way for Chalcedon, Theodore of Mopsuestia.

This they succeeded in doing, partly through misrepresentations of what Theodore really wrote. Under tremendous political pressure, Pope Vigilius, in 548, condemned specific writings of Theodore (and those of two of his associates) and then excommunicated him as a heretic. Five years later the Second Council of Constantinople (with the bishops also under great political pressure) upheld the condemnations. Even at the time, these actions were seen as contradictory to Chalcedon's declarations, and the Monophysites eventually ceased to be a force in the Church. Yet, they were the condemnations of a legitimate pope and a generally recognized ecumenical council.

Thus, Theodore's posthumous excommunication has remained one of those unfortunate incidents that occur in Church history. Most theologians today agree that nothing pronounced at the Second Council of Constantinople should be considered infallible, and all consider it a low point in the first millennium. Subsequent scholarship on Theodore (including the discovery of some of his writings previously unknown) has further vindicated his teaching. He is regularly cited for his positive contributions in finding a formula around which Christian generations to come could gather as they explored the essentially inexpressible mystery.

HINCMAR: VATICAN II PRECURSOR

A highly visible, outspoken figure in the Church during those years before the Dark Ages descended was Hincmar, archbishop of Reims in
France. His controversial theories about the relationship between pope
and bishops anticipated a major issue at the Second Vatican Council
by more than eleven hundred years. Hincmar's thirty-seven-year term
in office occurred during the second half of the ninth century as a series
of popes sought to make their authority over church and state more absolute. In the early part of the century the great emperor Charlemagne
had overseen everything affecting the governing of Christendom, including many aspects of Church life. With his passing, popes sought to
establish themselves as supreme arbiters. As Pope Nicholas I crowned
one of Charlemagne's successors, he presented the new emperor with
the sword as well, signifying that all power, spiritual and earthly, came
from the hands of the papacy. A later pope, John VIII, not only gave
Charles the Bald his crown and sword, but also selected this man to
be the new emperor. All the more did these popes exercise authority
in Church affairs, appointing bishops, issuing decrees and censures in
local matters, and intervening in disputes.

Hincmar was a metropolitan — that is, the archbishop of a major
diocese, one who traditionally possessed some limited jurisdiction over
other dioceses in the region, each headed by its own bishop. It was
Hincmar's bold contention that burgeoning papal absolutism represented an unfortunate infringement on the rights of local bishops
in general and metropolitans in particular. An expert in the ancient
canons on the subject, he argued that the universal Church had origi-
nally been conceived as an assembly of local churches that (under the
direction of the regional metropolitans) ran their own affairs and assembled from time to time in provincial councils to make decisions
or to issue directives for Christians in the area. On large, sweeping issues, he believed, decisions should come from general councils of all
the bishops. According to historian William La Due,

> [Hincmar] did not conceive of the unity of the Church in terms
> of its being a papal monarchy. Rather, he saw the universal
> Church as made up of an ensemble of local churches in com-
> munion with one another through a common faith and the

celebration of the Eucharist.... For him, the churches were ruled by the Scriptures, the canons of the great councils, and the norms that were generally accepted by the whole Church, and not by the personal authority of the bishop of Rome.[6]

Hincmar did not deny the primacy of the pope; rather, he saw papal authority as limited to applying the directives of councils and making alterations in keeping with changing times. His reasoning was based on the idea that Jesus appointed twelve apostles, giving each authority in his own right and reserving the Petrine authority to special situations.

Hincmar's influence in these matters might have carried more weight if he had been less absolutist in wielding authority in the dioceses he personally oversaw. He was continually at odds with Rome and with local bishops, some of whom would have preferred tyranny from Rome to tyranny from Reims. His influence was also limited by the impact that the discovery of the so-called Pseudo-Isidorian decretals had on the papacy. These largely forged documents (considered now among the most influential fabrications in history) portrayed the popes as far back as the first century as exercising absolute and unquestioned authority over the Church. Popes after Hincmar thereby felt reassured in their centralizing tendencies.

Nevertheless, the very debate Hincmar tried to generate actually took place a millennium later, when the bishops at Vatican II wrestled with the idea of episcopal collegiality. At issue was this question: Do bishops operate essentially as vicar-representatives of the pope or do they function in their own right as members of an empowered college? The direction of the Church in the nineteenth and early twentieth centuries suggested the former interpretation as the correct one. Yet in its Dogmatic Constitution on the Church (*Lumen Gentium*), the council endorsed the latter, more Hincmarian view:

Just as, by the Lord's will, St. Peter and the other apostles constituted one apostolic college, so in a similar way the Roman Pontiff as the successor of Peter, and the bishops as successors of the apostles are joined together....

The Church of Christ is truly present in all legitimate local congregations which, united with their pastors, are themselves called churches in the New Testament....

Bishops govern the particular churches...as the vicars and ambassadors of Christ.... This power, which they personally exercise in Christ's name, is proper, ordinary and immediate.... The pastoral office...is entrusted to them completely. Nor are they to be regarded as vicars of the Roman Pontiff, for they exercise authority which is proper to them and are quite properly called...heads of the people they govern.[7]

The full implementation of those concepts, as the Vatican II bishops realized and as subsequent events have indicated, may be a long time coming.

THOMAS AQUINAS: THE ARISTOTLE MYSTERY

More than seven hundred years after his birth, Thomas Aquinas is still universally regarded as one of the most influential thinkers in the history of Christianity. His creative blending of the faith of the Church with the philosophy of Aristotle has outlived dozens of other great systems of thought that have come and gone over the centuries. Even in a world of nuclear energy and space travel (or perhaps *especially* in such a world), millions find the insights of Thomas Aquinas inspiring and relevant. In his 1999 encyclical *Fides et ratio,* John Paul II joined dozens of his papal predecessors as he extolled Aquinas's "enduring originality": "In an age when Christian thinkers were rediscovering the treasures of ancient philosophy, and more particularly of Aristotle, Thomas had the great merit of giving pride of place to the harmony which exists between faith and reason."[8]

But what neither John Paul nor any of his predecessors have explained is how and why Thomas Aquinas, during his most creative years, publicly flaunted papal prohibitions against the teachings of Aristotle. No fewer than four popes and several provincial councils strictly banned works of the ancient philosopher throughout the thirteenth century. Yet Aquinas, as well as his mentor Albert the Great and other distinguished teachers of the time, cheerfully engaged in the work of applying the Aristotelian system to Christianity. This dissent from official papal teaching has been largely ignored by biographers of Aquinas, and even those who acknowledge the facts are hard-pressed to explain them. Says Thomistic historian Joseph Pieper, "I confess that I do not fully understand how this state of affairs was possible, either for the popes or for those wholly papal-minded monks."[9]

The facts are not in dispute. In 1210 the Council of Paris forbade the teaching of Aristotle's books of natural philosophy at the University of Paris, under pain of mortal sin. In 1215 legates of Pope Innocent III restated the prohibition. In 1228 Pope Gregory IX warned the theological faculty at Paris to cease and desist from using Aristotle's works. In 1231 Gregory reiterated this decision as binding until Aristotle's works were "purged of their errors." In 1245 Innocent IV extended the prohibition to the University of Toulouse and elsewhere. In 1263 Urban IV reminded the Church that the bans of Gregory were still in effect. Finally, in 1274 the archbishop of Paris excommunicated all those who taught certain Aristotelian-related propositions, some of which originated with Aquinas.[10]

In 1248 Thomas Aquinas was a Dominican seminarian in his early twenties studying at the University of Naples. It was there that he was introduced to the teachings of the ancient Greek philosopher by his teacher, Peter of Ireland. He then went to Paris, continuing his explorations under the guidance of Albert the Great. Aquinas's own notes of Albert's lectures on Aristotle's *Nichomachean Ethics* have been preserved, and in the first book that Aquinas himself wrote, on essence and existence, he referred consistently to Aristotle as *the* philosopher.

Obviously, the appeal of Aristotle to the people of the thirteenth century was strong. Observes Pieper,

> Something had been gestating within Western Christendom of the second millennium and was practically on the verge of seeing the light — a view of the universe and life that greatly resembled the Aristotelian view. This fellow Aristotle "suited" Western Christendom of around 1200 uncannily well; he offered to the Christian world the possibility of understanding itself. And so this new thing, like a wildly roaring torrent,... threatened to sweep away the dams and levees of tradition.[11]

That "something" gestating in Christendom was an interest in the world as it is. In previous centuries the emphasis had been on the transitory, temporary nature of the world; people were schooled to be indifferent to creatures, to value them only as shadows or symbols of eternal things. Thus, fire might be viewed as a symbol of God's power or as a spark of the divine light. But Aristotle argued persuasively that earthly things have value in themselves and should be studied and appreciated in their own light. He was more interested in what fire really is than in what it symbolized, and such thinking engaged the great minds of Italy, France, and England.

But the institutional Church, ever cautious of novel ideas, feared that all this would spark an epidemic of secularization and sinful worldliness. The great contribution of Aquinas, of course, was that he found a way to blend innovation and tradition, to honor creation in a worldly way without dishonoring or diminishing the Creator. As more than one commentator has noted, Aquinas baptized Aristotle.

How did Aquinas (and Albert and others) ignore clear Church law in apparently good conscience? Perhaps, says Pieper, Church authorities realized that these "warnings, restrictions, and prohibitions were a hopeless business from the start. . . . There is something strangely lackadaisical about these ordinances which were only spottily enforced."[12] When the University of Toulouse, for example, learned of the specific ban in Paris, it advertised its own Aristotelian courses all the more, which, after a considerable lapse of time, led to a specific (also largely ignored) ban at Toulouse as well. Another commentator, Martin Grabmann, suggests that the lucid teachings of Albert and Aquinas "practically abrogated" the Church's official rulings by the sheer force of their logic.[13] And Dominican theologian Thomas O'Meara says that the answer may lie in the fact that these teachings "transcended" the papal orders.[14] Yet, the authorities felt obligated to go through the motions, as it were, for more than seventy years.

In 1276, three years after Aquinas died at the age of forty-nine, the bishop of Paris, on orders from the pope, investigated these Aristotelian tendencies among theologians and subsequently condemned as erroneous and contrary to faith some two hundred propositions. He excommunicated (without naming names) all who taught them. Many of these were propositions found in the writings of Aquinas.

It is not clear when or if the bans were ever lifted. But time passed, and by 1366, some ninety years after the Paris excommunications, Thomistic-Aristotelian teaching was firmly entrenched in the major universities of Europe. Examining the situation at that time, legates of Pope Urban V decreed that, henceforth, anyone seeking the degree of licentiate in philosophy in the Catholic university would be required to pass an examination demonstrating a grasp of all the works of the great philosopher Aristotle.

The fame of Aquinas has continued to rise ever after. Said Pope John Paul,

> Profoundly convinced that whatever its source, truth is of the Holy Spirit,...St. Thomas was impartial in his love of truth. He sought truth wherever it might be found....In him the Church's Magisterium has seen and recognized the passion for truth; and precisely because it stays consistently within the horizon of universal, objective and transcendent truth, his thought scales heights "unthinkable to human intelligence."[15]

SOR JUANA: IN DEFENSE OF WOMEN

She has been called "the Mexican Muse," "the quasi-official poet of New Spain," and "the only great poet of the Spanish colonies in America."[16] Her plays, her spiritual writings, her scholarly monographs, and her sonnets have all been scrutinized and commented on by Hispanic scholars. But until recently, Sor (Sister) Juana Inés de la Cruz remained unknown in the English-speaking world.

She was a force of nature and she was a bundle of contradictions — a cloistered nun who moved freely in the court circles of viceroys and other nobility of Mexico City. She entertained them with a prodigious literary output; she could compose poetry about romantic love as easily as she probed the mysteries of the incarnation and the resurrection. She read voraciously — history, science, the ancient classics, the Fathers of the Church, and especially the Bible. And she seemed to retain almost everything she read, sprinkling her own writings with allusions that have sent many a reader searching for a dictionary — or a library. Yet, she was tortured by feelings of inferiority and worthlessness, never fully at peace with her marvelous talents.

Sor Juana's prominence as a nun and as a woman of letters in the male-dominated world of seventeenth-century Mexico sparked jealousy and animosity among many of her associates and some of her superiors. They had never seen anything like her before, nor would they see her like again. It was a peculiar manifestation of this opposition, a reproach from a bishop, that led Sor Juana to produce the work for which she is best known, *La Respuesta* (*The Response*), her intellectual autobiography. In it she presented a shockingly countercultural proclamation of the rights of women in the Church and in society. It was a bold move that caused her confessor to abandon her, a censor to label her impertinence heretical, and others to consider Sor Juana deserving of investigation by the Inquisition.

She was born in 1651 in a small town some fifty miles from Mexico City, the illegitimate child of a Creole woman and a Spanish military officer. She never knew her father, but she had the advantage of a caring mother, and a grandfather who possessed an enormous library. She taught herself to read at the age of three and could not stop. "In me the desire for learning was stronger than the desire for eating," she said.[17] She had no interest in marriage, and at the age of eighteen she entered a convent of the order of St. Jerome. At a time when the first pilgrims had barely arrived in North America and were battling the Indians, Mexico City was a flourishing cultural and religious center, with the convents of some sixteen orders of nuns.

Though cloistered, the St. Jerome sisters moved about freely, lived in their personal apartments at the convent, and interpreted the vow of poverty very broadly. Sor Juana's own library was said to number several thousand volumes.

In 1690 she was at the height of her abilities. Two of her books of poetry had been published in Spain, and she was continually in demand to write a libretto or compose a poem for some occasion of church or state. It happened that under discussion at the time was a famous sermon delivered by a Portuguese Jesuit forty years before. The subject of the talk—Christ's greatest "finesse" (that is, his greatest hidden manifestation of love)—was so esoteric and abstruse as to be incomprehensible to modern readers. Sor Juana considered the sermon illogical and wrote a lengthy refutation, her first venture into heavy theology. Though she did not intend it for publication, the bishop of Puebla had the work published anyway, commending her for the "energetic clarity" of her argument. In an astonishing turnaround, he then wrote her a letter, which was widely circulated, in which he forcefully reminded her of St. Paul's command in First Corinthians 14:34: "Let women be silent in church; they are not to be allowed to speak." He urged her to devote herself to religious study and the salvation of her soul, and to cease her other activities.

The letter apparently released a torrent of dammed up resentment in Sor Juana's soul. Her *Response* touched on many aspects of her life, but she especially challenged the accepted interpretation of St. Paul's command, viewing it as an excuse to degrade and exploit women.

She argued that it is not so much gender but incompetence that should prohibit one from speaking in church. "Not only women," she said, "but also men, who merely for being men believe they are wise, should be prohibited from interpreting the Sacred Word if they are not learned and virtuous and of gentle and well-inclined natures."[18] Noting that St. Paul called on everyone "not to be more wise than it behooves you to be wise," she wrote, "In truth, the Apostle did not direct these words to women, but to men; and *keep silence* is intended not only for women, but for all incompetents."

She wondered why such great stress was placed on one reference to silence in the Bible when there are many others, like "Hear, O Israel, and be silent." That, she noted, "addresses the entire congregation of men and women, commanding all to silence"; yet, it had never been understood as an absolute. Besides, wrote Sor Juana with interesting prescience, the choice of male or female nouns and pronouns throughout Scripture is somewhat arbitrary, as is "writing a plural for a singular or changing from the second to third persons." All this, she said, "demands more investigation than some, who strictly as grammarians...attempt to interpret the Scriptures, believe necessary."

She then took on the rigorists of her own day who said that Paul's silence referred to both silence in Church services and silence in *all* Church matters. What about the public teaching and writing of St. Teresa of Avila and St. Bridget of Sweden? she asked. "For if the Apostle had forbidden women to write, the Church would not have allowed it." And what about St. Jerome's disciple, Paula, "learned in Hebrew, Greek, and Latin, and most able in interpreting the Scriptures"? If Paul meant that women should neither speak publicly nor teach, how is it possible, she wondered, that this same Paul in his epistle to Titus urged older women to "teach well" those who are younger?

In her own studies, she said, she continually encountered women who were anything but silent: "I find Debbora administering the law, both military and political.... I find a most wise Queen of Sheba, so learned that she dares to challenge with hard questions the wisdom of the greatest of all wise men." She probed the ancient classics to produce people like "Zenobia, Queen of the Palmyrans, as wise as she was valiant," and "Nicostrate, framer of Latin verses and most erudite in Greek" — in short, "a great throng of women deserving to be named... celebrated and venerated."

Toward the end of *The Response,* she directly challenged the bishop of Puebla: "If, as the censor says, the letter [her refutation of the Jesuit's sermon] is heretical, why does he not denounce it?" But if she only did what was permitted regularly to men, she failed to understand his sharp putdown. "What then is the evil in my being a woman?" she asked.

More discussion and controversy followed Sor Juana's frank defense, but no formal action was taken against her. The whole episode left her exhausted. Aside from a few short articles, she never wrote again, and she gradually gave away all the books in her library. She completely abandoned the public life of Mexico City in favor of a strict convent life of prayer and, ironically, silence. In 1694, just four years after *The Response,* Sor Juana Inés de la Cruz, then forty-four, died — probably of smallpox — while caring for sick nuns at her convent. She left behind a great mass of literature, much of which has lately interested U.S. theologians and historians. In her abrupt silence and quick departure, she also left behind some unanswered questions.

THE BROTHERS PURCELL: SLAVERY NO MORE

On the eve of the American Civil War in the early 1860s, American Catholics were in virtually unanimous agreement on two points: slavery as a system was not intrinsically evil, and abolition (the governmental liberation of all slaves) was an unwise and unacceptable proposal. The Church's historical approach to this "peculiar institution" largely explains their attitude; slavery was always regarded as a regrettable but unavoidable condition of fallen human nature. Even

Thomas Aquinas, in the thirteenth century, recognized slavery as a traditional institution that could not be rooted out without tearing the social fabric. When Spain and Portugal were subduing the New World in the fifteenth and sixteenth centuries, no fewer than five popes gave representatives of these nations the right to capture nonbelievers and reduce them to a state of perpetual slavery.

This blanket acceptance of the system shifted gradually in succeeding centuries as the African slave trade — and its accompanying horrors — gained momentum and notoriety. In 1839 Pope Gregory XVI condemned the slave trade in absolute terms: "We do admonish and adjure...all believers in Christ...that no one hereafter may dare unjustly to molest Indians, Negroes, or other men of this sort; or to despoil them of their goods; or to reduce them to slavery."[19]

A prominent American bishop of that period, John England of Charleston, South Carolina, whose diocese covered three slave-holding states, quickly explained that the decree did not refer to slavery as such. In letters to the U.S. secretary of state, England said that "from the earliest days of Christianity, theologians had refrained from condemning the system as intrinsically evil or contrary to natural and divine law."[20] He added that Pope Gregory himself had endorsed that interpretation during a private meeting. No Catholic voices disputed his position.

The contention of the abolitionists that slavery should be banned altogether appeared especially abhorrent to newly arrived immigrants, especially those from Ireland. Struggling to obtain low-paying jobs in a hostile environment, they feared that an avalanche of newly freed slaves might strain the job market beyond its limits. They were inclined to agree with Bishop Joseph Fenwick of Boston, who outlined the Catholic position in the *Boston Pilot,* his diocesan paper:

> We are friends of well regulated freedom, and from our souls
> detest oppression....While we are convinced that no human
> institution is...exempt from defects, we must, to the credit of
> our Southern neighbors, say that...the slave of the South enjoys
> more comfort, is often more moral, and certainly more exempt
> from care, and the temptation to vice, than the free black or
> indigent white man of the North.[21]

Despite protests to the contrary, there was more than a little blatant racism in this antiabolition stance. The *Boston Pilot* commented in 1862, "The negro indeed is unfortunate, and the creature has the common rights of humanity living in his breast; but in the country of the whites where the labor of the whites has done everything, but his, nothing, and where the whites find it difficult to earn a subsistence, what right has the negro either to preference, or to equality, or to admission?"[22]

Almost every prominent American prelate justified slavery in one way or another prior to the Civil War. Archbishop Martin Spalding of Baltimore called it a "great social evil," but then explained that emancipation would result in "ruining the country and causing injury to the poor slaves themselves."[23] The illustrious and colorful archbishop of New York, John Hughes, claimed that those who would abolish slavery were in "need of a strait-jacket and the humane protection of a lunatic asylum." The faithful, he added, will never be persuaded to "forsake the wise and good old path of their Divine Master and His Church."[24] Seminary textbooks reflected the prevailing view. A moral theology book by Archbishop Francis Kenrick of Baltimore declared:

> Since this [slavery] is the state of affairs, nothing against the law must be attempted, neither anything by which the slaves might be set free, nor must anything be done or said that would make them bear the yoke with difficulty. But the prudence and the charity of the sacred ministers must be shown in this, so that the slaves, informed by Christian morals, might show service to their masters, venerating always God, the supreme Master of us all.[25]

Then, just as war hostilities escalated, a dissenting voice was heard. It came from two brothers, Archbishop John Purcell of Cincinnati and Fr. Edward Purcell, editor of the archdiocesan newspaper, the *Catholic Telegraph*. Abolition, said the archbishop in 1862 in a stunning, widely circulated sermon, was not only appropriate, but morally necessary. He lashed out at clerics for attempting "to sanctify the crying sin of the South in holding millions of human beings in spiritual and physical bondage." Catholicism as such, he declared, is and always was incompatible with slavery; and the time had come for the faithful to face this hard truth. His brother, in a series of editorials, similarly called on

Catholics to open their eyes. "There is no heavier calamity than slavery," he wrote. "It corrupts heart and soul, and we have no respect for the Christianity of any person who would wish to see it preserved; it can no longer be tolerated or rationalized."[26]

Both Purcells were immediately attacked by other editors for betraying their own people and turning against the uncontradicted teaching of the American hierarchy. Said the New York *Metropolitan Record,* "The Negro is what the Creator made him — not a rudimentary Caucasian, not a human being in the process of development, but a negro, and such he will be at the last day if the race is not extinct.... Abolition would be the worst evil to befall hard working Catholics, since an influx of negro labor would reduce them [whites] to a condition worse than that of European peasants."[27]

Not so, said editor Purcell. Let the slave system be abolished; only then can the problems of the freed slaves be "grappled with" in a way that protects the legitimate rights of both races.

This sudden, unexpected, contrarian view apparently served as a wake-up call for many American Catholics. According to historian Madeleine Hooke Rice,

> Support for the Purcells came from a variety of sources.... In Massachusetts an anonymous member of an East Boston parish penned an antislavery tract in which he undertook to prove that Catholic policy had always favored emancipation. From different parts of the North, messages of encouragement and congratulation poured in to the Telegraph. Members of the clergy, their scruples against abolitionism removed by the [ongoing] war, likewise endorsed the demise of slavery.[28]

With President Lincoln's declaration of the Emancipation Proclamation in 1863, this new momentum gathered steam. And by the end of the war in 1865, few apologists for slavery could be found in the U.S. Catholic population. Ironically, the message did not get to Rome immediately. An embarrassing statement by the Holy Office in 1866 repeated the old line: "Slavery itself... is not at all contrary to the natural and divine law.... For the sort of ownership which a slave owner has over a slave is understood as nothing other than the perpetual right of disposing of the work of a slave for one's own profit."[29]

Any lingering doubts, however, were laid to rest two years later, in 1888, when Pope Leo XIII said that all forms of slavery were morally reprehensible, must be abolished, and must have their roots destroyed. In his view, this position in no way contradicted previous Church teaching. Said the pope, "From the beginning almost nothing was more venerated in the Catholic Church ... than the fact that she looked to see slavery eased and abolished. ... She stood forth as a strenuous defender of liberty. ... Indeed the more slavery flourished from time to time, the more strenuously she strove to [liberate slaves]."[30]

STANDING FIRM

Mother Theodore Guerin

Here we consider three (of many) instances in history in which a committed Catholic rejected the orders of a high-ranking Church superior. At issue was not doctrine as such, but obedience.

MARY MACKILLOP: "THE EXCOMMUNICATED ONE"

These men felt intimidated by Mary's independent spirit and steely character and were moved to reassert their power and authority in destructive ways. They saw themselves as paternal figures, and Mary as a fragile, helpless woman who needed their guidance and protection — well-meant sentiments in what was, after all, an unashamedly patriarchal society — and could not cope when Mary began to think and act for herself.[1]

This brief, charitable assessment by Mary MacKillop's biographer, Lesley O'Brien, is difficult to contradict. There had to be some rational explanation for the unremitting opposition and rancor she sustained in her forty-two-year effort to help Australia's poorest citizens.

MacKillop, the eldest of eight children of Scottish immigrant parents, had just started a career as a teacher in 1866 when she met a priest from the Adelaide diocese, Julian Woods. A brilliant man with a captivating manner, he talked with her about the needs of the young Australian continent, whose population had tripled between 1850 and 1860 due to immigration. Neither church nor state could handle the incoming droves; poverty, illiteracy, and crime were rampant.

Woods discussed with MacKillop a grand plan: a religious order of women to serve the neediest through schools, orphanages, shelters for the homeless, and other charitable institutions; an order whose members would embrace poverty by refusing to own buildings or land, subsisting entirely on donations and small fees; an order that would make no distinctions between lay and teaching sisters; a continent-wide order under centralized self-government, answerable only to Rome and not under the authority of local diocesan bishops.

MacKillop enthusiastically concurred with Woods, who then drew up a constitution for the order, to be called the Institute of St. Joseph, and they received tentative approval to go ahead from Adelaide bishop Laurence Sheil. MacKillop was the first to make her vows, under the name Sister Mary of the Cross, an apt title in view of subsequent developments. The community's growth rate was astonishing: from one member in 1867, to 30 sisters in 8 schools or institutions the next year, to 127 sisters (plus three dozen novices) operating in 17 locations by 1869. The growth, historians have claimed, can be explained in part by Woods's charismatic personality and in part by the dearth of opportunity for young women in the secular world at the time; many were attracted to this exciting, new, homegrown religious community. All went well at first, though MacKillop, as the twenty-five-year-old mother general, was swamped with administrative duties.

Woods's involvement with the institute continued for many years, but it was sprinkled with frequent conflicts and misunderstandings. He displayed odd tendencies, incurring huge debts on behalf of the order, admitting recruits without input from the sisters' council, and publicizing the activities of two sisters who claimed mystical experiences, including physical assaults by Satan.

In 1871, just four years after the foundation, Bishop Sheil formally objected to the institute he had endorsed: "I am going to have new Rules with lay and teaching sisters. . . . Every convent will be under the control of the local pastor — no other authority to appeal to except myself. There will be no Sister Guardian, no head but myself." Mac-

Killop replied, "Such an arrangement would be quite opposed to the Rule. I could not in conscience remain under those changes."[2]

In September a delegate of the bishop unexpectedly ordered Mac-Killop to depart the next day for an outlying region. Believing the bishop was poised to impose his changes and did not want her around, she refused to leave without first meeting with him. Early the next morning, Sheil, fully vested, with miter on head and crosier in hand, and accompanied by four priests, arrived at the sisters' house in Adelaide. He gathered the community together, ordered MacKillop to kneel before him, and pronounced sentence:

> Sister Mary of the Cross, Superior of the Institute of St. Joseph, on account of your disobedience and rebellion, I pronounce on you the awful sentence of excommunication. You are now Mary MacKillop, free to return to the world, a large portion of the wickedness of which you have, I fear, brought with you into this Institute.[3]

One of the sisters screamed in near hysteria, while others wept or fell on their knees. MacKillop later wrote about her immediate reaction: "I do not know how to describe the feeling but . . . I was intensely happy and felt nearer to God than I had ever felt before. . . . I cannot describe the calm beautiful something that was near."[4]

She rose and walked silently out of the house. In the next few days forty-seven of the forty-nine Adelaide sisters left their positions. Dressed as laywomen, they obtained food and shelter from supporters, including several Jewish and Protestant families. A scattering of friendly priests assured MacKillop that the excommunication was invalid, and appeals were dispatched to Rome, seeking an investigation. Sheil, who was in declining health, took no further action to impose his will on the order. Five months later, on his deathbed, the bishop revoked the excommunication. MacKillop and the others calmly donned their religious garb and went back to work.

Convinced that such difficulties would continue unless the institute's constitution received official approval from the Vatican, Mac-Killop spent most of the next two years in Europe raising funds and finally obtaining Rome's approbation for centralized self-government. She also had an audience with Pope Pius IX, who gave her special attention when his secretary introduced MacKillop as "the excommunicated one."

Upon returning to Australia, she quickly discovered that the problems would not go away, despite support from Rome. Irish-born Bishop Matthew Quinn of Bathurst, where the St. Joseph sisters were especially active in schools and orphanages, wrote to contacts in the Vatican, "Anything so unsuited to Australia as nuns formed on these Rules can hardly be conceived. . . . I will form my own subjects according to the necessities of my own diocese."[5] After extended efforts to placate the bishop, MacKillop withdrew her sisters from the diocese.

The bishop's brother, Bishop James Quinn of Brisbane, made strenuous efforts over a period of years to revise the St. Joseph constitution so that the sisters in his diocese would be directly under his jurisdiction. MacKillop told him that she would pull everyone out if he persisted. He did and, eventually, she did. For years he deluged Rome with letters about this band of rebellious, self-willed nuns.

Back at the institute's headquarters in Adelaide, Sheil's successor, Bishop Christopher Reynolds, undertook an episcopal "visitation" to determine if the sisters were in full compliance with Church law. Selected sisters were quizzed about the order's finances and especially about rumors that Mother MacKillop was an alcoholic. The sisters were put under oath never to reveal anything that had been discussed. At the conclusion of this visitation, Reynolds claimed he had "instructions" from Rome to ban MacKillop from his diocese: "I therefore notify your Maternity to prepare to leave . . . as you no longer have the confidence of the sisterhood."[6] She moved to Sidney and contacted Rome, only to learn that no instructions had been issued. When the Adelaide sisters were later absolved of their oath of silence, it was revealed that none had accused MacKillop of alcoholism, though many said that Reynolds's inquisitors had tried to persuade them to accuse her.

In the years that followed, MacKillop continued to be dogged by complaints from bishops and priests. And in 1885 the Australian bishops at their annual meeting voted, fourteen to three, to revoke the institute's self-governing provision. It required three more years of turmoil before MacKillop persuaded Vatican officials to allow self-government to stand.

During all this turmoil, the institute continued to grow and flourish, extending its operations to almost every diocese of Australia and to New Zealand, and eventually returning to Bathurst and Brisbane. In 1899 MacKillop, now sixty years old and suffering from multiple sclerosis, suffered a stroke that left her physically, but not mentally, incapacitated until her death in 1908.

She was survived by a religious family of 750 sisters educating twelve thousand students across the continent and operating dozens of charitable institutions. Something about MacKillop's unwavering perseverance resonated with Australians, and in the twentieth century she became something of a national heroine. Multiple biographies were written and a popular movie of her life, *Mary*, was widely circulated. In Rome in 1995, following a lengthy investigation of her life by Church officials, Pope John Paul II declared her blessed and worthy of veneration.

GROSSTESTE: "I DO NOT OBEY"

In the year 1253 Pope Innocent IV ordered the bishop of Lincoln in England to appoint the pope's nephew to a position as canon in the cathedral at Lincoln. The nephew, Frederick of Lavagna, did not intend to move to England or undertake any duties as canon; he would simply receive regular financial benefits from his position. Such appointments of absentee canons were commonplace in the thirteenth century, and no pope was more profligate in handing out these positions to relatives and friends than Innocent IV. The income, which the beneficiary would naturally share with the pope, helped to support papal causes, including an endless war with Frederick II.

The bishop of Lincoln, Robert Grossteste, refused the pope's command in an impassioned letter that has amazed and puzzled scholars since:

> Because of the obedience by which I am bound to the Apostolic See... filially and obediently, I do not obey, I oppose, I rebel. You cannot take any action against me for my every word and act is not rebellion but the filial honour due by God's command to father and mother. As I have said, the Apostolic See in its holiness

cannot destroy, it can only build. This is what the plenitude of power means; it can do all things for edification. But these so-called provisions do not build up, they destroy.[7]

It was commonly accepted in those times that the pope's "plenitude of power" meant that he was to be obeyed unconditionally, even if his command represented an unjust abuse of power. The pope was seen as standing supreme on earth in the place of Jesus Christ; only the arrogant and disobedient would dare dispute such eminence. On what grounds, then, could Grosseteste, recognized universally as a conscientious bishop and an exceptionally holy man, simply refuse to obey — and with such defiance?

That question energized numerous historians in the nineteenth century, and they were able to come up with two possible answers: either the bishop let his emotions get the better of him and he was therefore not an obedient Catholic, or he did not write the letter attributed to him. Historian F. W. Maitland opted for the first explanation but was troubled by it: "The more we make of Grosseteste's heroism in withstanding Innocent IV the worse we think of his logical position. And bad enough it was. He had conceded to the apostolic see a power of freely dealing out ecclesiastical benefices all the world over and then had to contend that this should be used but not abused."[8] Another commentator, Charles Jourdain, disputed the letter's authenticity, but later research has established that the document was authentic and written in Grosseteste's hand.

There the question lay, unresolved until a more extensive analysis was done in the 1960s by Brian Tierney, a historian of Church laws and decrees. Tierney argued that Grosseteste was well within his rights (as understood in the thirteenth century) when he confronted the pope. The accepted canon law of the time, he demonstrated, recognized limits to the papal "plenitude." Yes, said the canonists, the "apostolic see" has been granted divine authority; but no, not every command of every pope necessarily has the support of this authority. Hence, said Tierney, the bishop of Lincoln's appeal to the apostolic see was quite appropriate: "And this led him to his concluding declaration that, precisely in order to remain loyal and obedient to the apostolic see, it was necessary for him to disobey that particular command of the pope."[9]

What made the appointment of absentee canons so deplorable and unacceptable, Grosseteste declared in his letter, was its result — the injury, the tearing down, the destruction of the good of the Church. Tierney showed that, ironically, Innocent himself, the pope whose order was so vehemently challenged, actually agreed in principle with Grosseteste. In his own commentaries the pope acknowledged limits to papal power. If, for example, a pope ordered a monk to violate his vows, Innocent wrote, the monk ought not obey. And, he added, if the pope ordered something "injurious" to the "state of the Church," one would be justified in resisting. Thus, concludes Tierney,

> [The bishop] was a profoundly Catholic pastor of souls; and he was never more Catholic than when he refused to injure the Church at the behest of the Pope. In disobeying Innocent IV, Grosseteste was neither rejecting his own inner convictions in a moment of anger nor formulating a novel principle of resistance to papal authority. He was acting in accordance with a widely accepted and well-developed doctrine of the Church.[10]

Innocent was well aware of Grosseteste's concerns about the good of the Church. The bishop had earlier traveled to Rome to discuss what he regarded as serious abuses in the Curia. He told Innocent that "the Curia choked the system with privileges, exemptions, the creation of legal tangles, the tolerance of evils and active support of evil-doers, in order to forward the family interests and political ambitions of the pope and cardinals." Curia members, he charged, were "worse than those who crucified Christ," since the latter did not know what they were doing, while the Curia's policies promoted "the destruction of souls, a contempt for eternity and the glorification of transitory things."[11]

That visit to Rome had no known effect on curial policy, nor did Grosseteste's letter have any affect on Innocent's determination to assist a relative. Bypassing this rebellious bishop, the pope wrote to the papal legate in England and the archdeacon of Canterbury, commanding that his nephew be declared a canon in Lincoln and provided with the required remuneration. He also declared null and void in advance any resistance from any source.

How Grosseteste accepted this outcome is not known. He remained as bishop until his death. Afterwards, there were reports of miracles at his tomb, and supporters pressed for his canonization. Rome, however, declined to pursue the matter.

MOTHER GUERIN: COURAGE UNDER FIRE

In September of 1844 Mother Theodore Guerin returned to Vincennes, Indiana, with a sense of foreboding. She had been away for almost a year raising funds in Europe for the schools that she and a handful of other Sisters of Providence had established during the previous four years. The task had not been an easy one. Vincennes was a sprawling diocese where settlers were hewing farms and villages out of the fields and forests of the fertile southwest Indiana land. The sisters had come from France at the request of the Vincennes bishop, Celestine de la Hailandiere. Less than 20 percent of Indiana's children attended any school, he had explained to Mother Mary Lecor, superior general of the Sisters of Providence, a fast-growing order of nuns dedicated to "the instruction of young girls and the care of the unfortunate."

So Guerin and five other sisters had been dispatched into the wild, with little knowledge of the people and less of the English language. Guerin was forty-two years old at the time and in chronically poor health. Yet, in those four years, despite inclement weather and a fire that destroyed their crops, they had made progress. Near Terre Haute, Indiana, they had opened a boarding school at St. Mary-of-the-Woods. This became the community's headquarters and the novitiate for recruits to the order. They had also set up mission schools in three nearby towns, all with rapidly growing enrollments.

What concerned Guerin upon her return was the decision by Mother Mary Lecor and other Church officials to separate this American branch of the order from the foundation in France. Though still following the rules of the Sisters of Providence, they would be self-governing, essentially self-supporting, and under the authority of the bishop of Vincennes. Bishop Hailandiere, supportive of the sisters at the beginning, had recently shown severely autocratic tendencies. Guerin did not know what to expect now that he was the sisters' duly appointed overseer.

She found out soon enough. During her absence (and without any input from the sisters), he had admitted several novices into the order, closed one of the mission schools and assigned the nuns elsewhere, and admitted two women from another order into the Providence community. He had also called for the election of a new superior, but the community sisters had unanimously reelected Guerin, much to Hailandiere's chagrin. During a two-hour welcome-home harangue, he told Guerin that he was now officially in charge, and accused her of stealing money from him while in Europe and plotting against him.

At the time, the sisters needed a larger facility for the boarding school. The bishop told them to build a school at their own expense on a parcel of land he owned. Guerin proposed the idea to the community, and all the members flatly refused, which led to another unpleasant encounter with Hailandiere. Guerin said that they would under no circumstances build on land they did not own, and reminded him that he had not yet, as their ecclesiastical overseer, approved their religious rule. She later wrote, "He told me the community was his and that it would always remain his, that if I were not content I could leave alone and at once if I wished; he added emphatically as he pointed out to me our little cabin [the sisters' house]: 'I am the proprietor, spiritual and temporal, of that house; I am going to forbid you to set foot in it.' The good God gave me the grace to remain calm. Little by little Monsignor [the bishop] calmed down."[12]

The harassment continued, and Guerin began to think that perhaps "the moment has come when we must leave the distressing state in which we have been for so long a time" and return to France.[13] But she worried about the American novices who had joined the order. "The mere idea of leaving them bruises our hearts," she said. Then she added, "I have interiorly the confidence that the good God wishes us in America. If he wished to destroy us, would he send us so many crosses — that precious cross which has always been the seal of his works?"

The months of deadlock turned into years, the bishop continuing to withhold approval of the community's rule and making every effort to oust Guerin. On one occasion he yielded a bit, offering the sisters the deed for the land on which to build an expanded school, but adding that he would have to approve every detail of construction and every aspect of its operation when completed. Guerin and the community rejected the offer under such conditions.

It has never been made clear what prompted Hailandiere's animosity toward Guerin, though he once wrote that he did not believe a "country girl" like Guerin had the proper disposition to head "a congregation of submissive daughters who will have the spirit of God." The situation in Indiana, however, was not unique. Throughout the nineteenth century similar problems between women religious and local bishops—especially French bishops—were reported in newly settled areas of the United States.

The climax occurred in May of 1847. Guerin had just returned from a tour of six mission schools and stopped at Vincennes to see the bishop. He demanded, under holy obedience, that she resign immediately, and she refused. He locked her in a room at his residence and went out to dinner. When some of the sisters came looking for her late in the evening, he let her out, and then went to the sisters' house with a solemn decree: Guerin was no longer superior of the community and was, in fact, dismissed from the Sisters of Providence. Her vows were revoked; she must leave Indiana immediately "to hide her disgrace," and she was forbidden to communicate with anyone in the community.

The sisters at Vincennes defied him to his face, saying they would not yield to a dictator. Hailandiere then contacted the sisters living at St. Mary-of-the-Woods with an offer that was explained to them by one of their associates: "Monsignor has said that he would excommunicate all the sisters who would leave his diocese without permission. He will not let them take away the least thing and perhaps will have them followed by the police. On the contrary, those who remain will have the land of St. Mary-of-the-Woods and the protection of their bishop together with his confidence."

None accepted the offer, and all began to pack without any idea where they could go. Meanwhile, Guerin, who became seriously ill, remained in Vincennes. She later wrote that she thought that she was dying and asked the Vincennes vicar general to come and hear her confession. He refused, but a newly ordained priest (who happened to be Hailandiere's nephew) did respond. "I had been banished," she wrote. "I was ill without asylum, without money, without protector; the month of Mary was approaching its end; it was May 30."

Then suddenly, out of the blue, came deliverance. More than two years before, Hailandiere, in a depressed mood, had written to Rome, offering to resign. The offer was rejected then. Now came a letter saying that the Congregation of Bishops not only accepted his offer, but also had already appointed a priest, John Bazin, as his immediate replacement.

The community rejoiced, and Mother Guerin, amazingly recuperated, came home to St. Mary-of-the-Woods on the steamboat *Daniel Boone* a few days after the announcement. A crowd of cheering townspeople met her at the dock, and the city canons of Terre Haute were fired to herald the victory. Bazin, in a letter, likened Hailandiere to Don Quixote tilting at windmills, and said he was to be pitied. He gave the community full cooperation and freedom — as did his successors.

These trials were over, and the Sisters of Providence flourished in the years ahead in Indiana, Illinois, and other states. Guerin continued as superior until her death at fifty-seven in 1856, just nine years after Hailandiere's departure. A flood of tributes arrived from former students, associates, and Church officials in America and in France, and the cause of her canonization began in the early 1900s. She was designated as venerable in 1992, and Pope John Paul II declared her blessed in 1998, the last step prior to proclamation as a saint.

COSTLY FIDELITY

The expression "faithful dissent" is not an oxymoron; history says that loud and clear. The people described in these chapters took risky stands and sometimes paid heavily for their audacity. Yet, the benefits of their dissent have unquestionably enriched the Church. These dissenters challenged fossilized traditions and seemingly irreformable doctrines, opened locked windows, and pushed the Church (sometimes kicking and screaming) into the future. The cases presented here by no means exhaust the inventory of such dissent to be found in Church archives; they represent but the tip of the iceberg. If cases of responsible dissent seem unfamiliar or exceptional, it is due in large part to the institutional Church's reluctance to acknowledge, much less celebrate, them. Institutional leaders do not like to admit error and have sometimes tried to rewrite history in order to escape embarrassment — always at the expense of institutional credibility.

Are there common threads running through these instances of dissent that might be instructive for those struggling with contemporary, unresolved matters of dissent? Though each situation has unique characteristics that make generalization or cataloging difficult, there certainly are commonalities.

In many cases reported in this book the dissenter or dissenters were actually the advocates for a common perception or a new understanding that had already taken root in the Catholic community; they were neither inventors nor lone rangers. The dispute over usury is a relatively clear example. Here the Jesuits, other theologians, and concerned laity tried to bring Church doctrine into conformity with changes in the European economic system already in wide acceptance but condemned by the hierarchy. The Jesuits served as critical spokespersons and apologists for the system that was ultimately accepted.

Similarly, Galileo was the voice for new information about the nature of the universe that was gradually being received into the scientific community. In this role, he made extraordinary attempts to reconcile the new science with the old faith, formulating principles concerning the interpretation of Scripture and tradition that eventually opened the Church to new vistas of self-understanding, as Pope John Paul II once noted (though they did not save Galileo from a forced repudiation).

Likewise, John Courtney Murray, in his long crusade against the traditional church-state doctrine, did not operate simply out of personal conviction; rather, he articulated in nuanced theological language what American Catholics had been experiencing for almost two hundred years — namely, that the separation of church and state is advantageous, not detrimental, to organized religion. It was an idea that contradicted centuries of European practice; hence, its recognition was hard earned through costly dissent.

In the above three instances the struggle for change was particularly rancorous because the doctrines in dispute had been presented by the Church as definitive, fixed, and irreformable. The magisterium did not believe that it was authorized to alter them. Only in retrospect, after the change occurred, did the whole Church, from bottom to top, see that these doctrines had been in development and subject to change because of new information or insight.

John Henry Newman's case has special relevance here because he established the appeal to the sense of the faithful as a critical factor in resolving disputes. He did this by pointing to a dramatic fourth-century situation in which the laity's determination prevailed over a widespread hierarchical surrender to heresy.

Similar dynamics may have been at work in the dissent of Thomas Aquinas, Albert the Great, and others over the teaching of Aristotle in universities. They acted in keeping with a wide, growing conviction among Catholics of the time that the ancient philosopher had treasures to impart to Catholic thought. In this sense, it would appear that Church authority was out of sync with the larger Christian community, and it took almost a century for the Church's official teachers to catch up with the pupils.

The work of Matteo Ricci and his successors in China represents a variation on this theme of the sense of the faithful. Vastly separated from central authorities in Rome both in miles and in opportunities to communicate, they made radical, noncanonical adaptations of Catholic teaching and terminology to the existing religious experience and practice of the Chinese people. They operated out of their own prayerful judgment about what was appropriate and out of a conviction, now accepted by Catholicism, at least in theory, that a certain vestigial sense of the faithful exists in the not-yet faithful.

Lest one be tempted to see every form of responsible dissent as an expression of some Catholic consensus, consideration must be given to the issue of slavery. Before the American Civil War, there existed among American Catholics a strong sense that slavery was morally permissible, a sense shared equally by clergy and laity. That sense was wrongheaded. Opposition to slavery came from certain Protestant groups, and Catholics generally resented their stand. As it turned out, this Catholic approbation of slavery was broad but not deep, and it virtually disappeared when a few dissenting voices (bolstered by a presidential edict) spoke up. Today, the Church universal agrees that slavery is — and always was — intrinsically evil.

Yves Congar's career as a promoter of ecumenism also suggests that the sense of the faithful might be a more useful concept if it included — at least in some situations — the sense of non-Catholic Christians. The push for dialogue and cooperation among churches came almost exclusively from the Protestant side. Congar's involvement in the movement despite Church disapproval immersed him in continual trouble for many years.

Other expressions of responsible dissent have roots in pastoral needs of the Catholic community that were not being met. This is particularly true with Mary Ward's Institute of the Blessed Virgin Mary and Mary MacKillop's Institute of St. Joseph, though they are separated by three hundred years and thousands of miles. In both cases the founders were moved to extend schooling and other services to a neglected clientele. Ward simply ignored canonical impediments, and MacKillop stoutly resisted a barrage of hierarchical takeovers. Mother Theodore Guerin's dissent from the orders of her bishop was also founded in a deep commitment to provide needed ministry. It is no mere coincidence that women's dissent is more often related to pastoral and educational situations. Barred from direct input in the development of doctrine and Church governance, women turned to direct service, occasionally clashing with authority. The canonization process underway for all three of these sisters testifies to the Church's overall assessment of their contributions.

Catherine of Siena is so unique that she resists categorization under known labels. Yet, it might be argued that in her single-minded determination to bring the papacy back to Rome ("Do God's will and mine!"), she represented a broad sense of the faithful as well as the pastoral needs of her age. It was becoming increasingly clear that the long papal sojourn in Avignon was producing ecclesiastical catastrophe.

Then there are those instances of dissent that seem to originate totally in the inspiration of a single individual and are completely disassociated from cultural norms. Prominent here is the creation-centered, feminist-oriented theology of Hildegard of Bingen. It came to her, she said, through the "Living Light," and it escaped notice (and likely condemnation) because it was so far ahead of eleventh-century conventions as to be unintelligible to censors or inquisitors.

Like Hildegard in some respects is Sor Juana Inés de la Cruz, whose insights into Scripture and culture transcended her seventeenth-century milieu. Unlike Hildegard, her dissent was easier to understand, and she suffered accordingly.

•

In two important respects the dissenters described here are unqualifiedly alike. First, they absolutely refused to leave the Church in the face of all their difficulties. One could argue that this stubborn fidelity, this standing in place while contradicting authority, was the principal factor in their ultimate success and (sometimes posthumous) vindication. Second, they did not see themselves as disobedient persons. They shared a remarkable awareness that submission to God and submission to Church authority are not always the same thing. Some today might call them "cafeteria Catholics." In a sense, they were; they maintained that not everything in the cafeteria was edible. Nevertheless, their acknowledgement of Church authority and their gratitude for what the Church offered them over the long haul never left. Congar perhaps put it best when he said near the end of his often troubled career, "The Church is the hearth of my soul. . . . She offers me the possibility of living with the saints; and when did she ever prevent me from living a Christian life?"[1]

•

If there is a patron saint for responsible dissenters, I would like to propose Job, that grievously afflicted, extremely articulate figure of the Old Testament. The book of Job is quite complex, and among its messages is that one may vigorously disagree even with God and get a hearing. At first glance, Job may not seem a suitable patron, since he does not get all the answers he wants. But there's more to Job's story than first meets the eye.

First, Job has a most curious mind. He wants to know what's going on and he wants to know why. "I shall say to God, 'Do not condemn me, but tell me the reason for your assault. Is it right for you to injure me, cheapening the work of your own hands?'"

Second, he does not easily accept traditional explanations. Though he listens to those proposed by the verbose authority figures who visit him, he expresses his disagreement in the most forceful terms. "I wish someone would teach you to be quiet.... Kindly listen to my accusation, pay attention to the pleading of my lips."

Third, throughout his entire ordeal Job never loses his faith; his protests, loud and long, are always channeled through unshakable belief. "I cry to you and you give me no answer; I stand before you and you take no notice. You have grown cruel in your dealings with me, and your hand lies on me, heavy and hostile."

Finally, Job wins! Toward the end of the book, authority figure Elihu tells Job to give it up: God is God and human words are not likely to reach his ear. "Clothed in fearful splendor," says Elihu, God does not respond to mere mortals. And just like that, five lines later, God appears "from the heart of the tempest." And God responds! He gives Job a one-on-one glimpse of his splendor. At last Job has made contact; he finally rests easy. "Now I see you with my own eyes," he says.[2]

In his book *The First Dissident,* William Safire finds abundant inspiration in this most mysterious figure out of the ancient past. What Safire says about those who challenge God would surely apply all the more to those who dare challenge God's representatives in the Church:

Modesty and reverence are fine human traits, and befit a philosophy that accepts the inaccessibility of wisdom and the un-
knowability of God.... But Job teaches that the arrogance of
moral outrage is divinely, not diabolically, inspired.... This challenge by an argumentative believer led to contact with the deity,
and the content of that contact, intuitively understood, led to his
reaffirmation of faith.... [The book] was propagating an idea of
particular interest to the open minded: Those needing to engage
with God...are most able to come to "see" God, however awe-
some or intimidating that insight turns out to be. As a basis for
worship, awe is better than fear, and the need to engage is best
of all. Job refused to quit protesting until he was permitted to
see—that is, to get a quick peek, a metaphysical teaser, at a corner of all he is yet to learn. God may take offense at disrespect,
and if he chooses to reveal himself you'll soon know that, but
he is more profoundly offended at phony piety — unthinking
or wrongheaded orthodoxy. Skeptics catch the divine drift: You
may or may not find the answer by demanding to know, but you
will surely never find the answer by fearing to ask.[3]

NOTES

INTRODUCTION

1. William Gibson, *The Miracle Worker* (New York: Atheneum, 1960), 276–77.

1. JOHN COURTNEY MURRAY

1. Cited in Donald E. Pelotte, *John Courtney Murray: Theologian in Conflict* (New York: Paulist Press, 1976), 148.

2. Cited in ibid., 17.

3. The Murray-Bowie debate is cited in ibid., 18–19.

4. The Fenton-Murray controversy is cited in ibid., 160–63.

5. Murray's position is cited in detail in J. Leon Hooper and Todd David Whitmore, eds., *John Courtney Murray and the Growth of Tradition* (Kansas City: Sheed & Ward, 1996), 142–44.

6. Cited in Pelotte, *John Courtney Murray,* 167.

7. Cited in ibid., 168.

8. Cited in ibid., 38.

9. Quotations in this section are cited in ibid., 37–52.

10. Ibid., 47.

11. Cited in ibid., 171.

12. Quotations in this section are cited in ibid., 52–59.

13. Quotations in this section are cited in ibid., 75–76, 109.

14. Quotations in this section are cited in ibid., 79–87.

15. Quotations in this section are cited in ibid., 96–98.

16. Ibid., 99.

17. "Declaration on Religious Freedom," in *The Documents of Vatican II,* ed. Walter M. Abbott (New York: America Press, 1966), nos. 2, 4, 11.

18. Cited in Pelotte, *John Courtney Murray,* 101.

19. John Courtney Murray, "Freedom in the Age of Renewal," *American Benedictine Review* (September 1967): 320.

20. Tributes are cited in Pelotte, *John Courtney Murray,* 105–6.

2. GALILEO

1. Cited in Maurice A. Finnocchiaro, ed. and trans., *The Galileo Affair: A Documentary History* (Berkeley: University of California Press, 1989), 30.

2. Cited in ibid., 49–50.

3. Cited in ibid., 35.

4. Cited in ibid., 146.

5. Cited in ibid., 214–16.

6. Cited in ibid., 217–18.

7. Cited in ibid., 229–32.

8. Cited in ibid., 264–68.

9. Cited in ibid., 148.

10. Cited in ibid., 276.

11. Cited in ibid., 278.

12. Cited in ibid., 287.

13. Cited in ibid., 291.

14. James Orgren, "Galileo and the Church: Then and Now" (unpublished manuscript, 1988), 26.

15. Cited in Finnocchiaro, ed. and trans., *The Galileo Affair,* 292–93.

16. Orgren, "Galileo and the Church," 26.

17. Cited in J. J. Fahie, *Galileo, His Life and Work* (London: John Murray, 1903), 339–40.

18. Cited in ibid., 403.

19. Orgren, "Galileo and the Church," 30.

20. Jerome Langford, *Galileo, Science, and the Church* (Ann Arbor: University of Michigan Press, 1966), 177–78.

21. Cited in Orgren, "Galileo and the Church," 33.

22. Pope John Paul II, *Fides et ratio,* nos. 16, 34.

3. JOHN HENRY NEWMAN

1. Cited in Christopher Hollis, *Newman and the Modern World* (London: Hollis & Carter, 1967), 61.

2. Cited in John Henry Newman, *On Consulting the Faithful in Matters of Doctrine,* ed. John Coulson (London: Collins Liturgical Press, 1986), 8.

3. Cited in ibid., 18.

4. Cited in ibid., 84.

5. Cited in ibid., 91.

6. Cited in ibid., 77.

7. Cited in Richard R. Gaillardetz, *Witnesses to the Faith: Community, Infallibility, and the Ordinary Magisterium of Bishops* (New York: Paulist Press, 1992), 66–68.

8. Cited in Newman, *On Consulting the Faithful,* 63.

9. Cited in ibid.

10. Cited in ibid., 76.

11. Cited in ibid., 31.

12. Cited in ibid., 35.

13. Cited in Hollis, *Newman and the Modern World,* 128.

14. Cited in Newman, *On Consulting the Faithful,* 38.

15. Cited in ibid., 41.

16. Cited in ibid., 43.

17. Cited in ibid., 44.

18. Cited in Hollis, *Newman and the Modern World,* 213.

19. Francis Aloysius Sullivan, *Magisterium: Teaching Authority in the Catholic Church* (New York: Paulist Press, 1983), 104.

20. "Dogmatic Constitution on the Church," in *The Documents of Vatican II,* ed. Walter M. Abbott (New York: America Press, 1966), nos. 12, 35.

21. "Decree on the Apostolate of the Laity," in Abbott, ed., *The Documents of Vatican II,* nos. 2, 3.

22. Hollis, *Newman and the Modern World,* 180.

23. Cited in ibid., 127.

4. MARY WARD

1. Cited in Jeanne Cover, *Love — the Driving Force: Mary Ward's Spirituality* (Milwaukee: Marquette University Press, 1997), 83.

2. Cited in ibid., 175.

3. Cited in Jo Ann McNamara, *Sisters in Arms: Catholic Nuns through the Millennia* (London: Harvard University Press, 1996), 462.

4. Cited in Cover, *Love — the Driving Force,* 58.

5. McNamara, *Sisters in Arms,* 462.

6. Cited in Cover, *Love — the Driving Force,* 58.

7. Cited in ibid., 60.

8. Citations and quotations in this section are in ibid., 26–27.

9. Except where otherwise noted, quotations in this section are cited in ibid., 18–29.

10. Cited in ibid., 145.

11. Cited in ibid., 125.

12. Cited in ibid., 165.

13. Cited in ibid., 53.

14. Cited in McNamara, *Sisters in Arms,* 463.

15. Cited in Cover, *Love — the Driving Force,* 170.

16. Cited in ibid., 129.

17. Cited in ibid., 18.

18. Cited in ibid., 130.

19. Cited in ibid., 9.

20. "Decree on the Appropriate Renewal of the Religious Life," in *The Documents of Vatican II,* ed. Walter M. Abbott (New York: America Press, 1966), no. 2.

21. Cited in Cover, *Love — the Driving Force,* 129.

5. THE JESUITS AND USURY

1. Cited in Maureen Fiedler and Linda Rabben, eds., *Rome Has Spoken: A Guide to Forgotten Papal Statements and How They Have Changed through the Centuries* (New York: Crossroad, 1998), 198.

2. Cited in ibid., 199.

3. Cited in John T. Noonan Jr., "The Amendment of Papal Teaching," in *Contraception: Authority and Dissent,* ed. Charles E. Curran (New York: Herder and Herder, 1969), 42.

4. Cited in ibid., 49.

5. Cited in ibid.

6. Cited in ibid., 58.

7. Cited in ibid.

8. Cited in ibid., 74.

9. Ibid., 64.

10. Cited in ibid., 66.

11. Cited in ibid., 55.

12. Cited in Fiedler and Rabben, eds., *Rome Has Spoken,* 201.

13. Cited in ibid.

14. Noonan, "The Amendment of Papal Teaching," 75.

6. CATHERINE OF SIENA

1. Barbara W. Tuchman, *A Distant Mirror: The Calamitous Fourteenth Century* (New York: Knopf, 1978), 28.

2. Ibid., 251.

3. Cited in Anthony Butkovich, *Revelations: Saint Birgitta of Sweden* (Los Angeles: Ecumenical Foundation of America), 72.

4. Carol Lee Flinders, *Enduring Grace: Living Portraits of Seven Women Mystics* (San Francisco: HarperSanFrancisco, 1993), 116.

5. Cited in Johannes Jørgensen, *Saint Catherine of Siena,* trans. Ingeborg Lund (New York: Longmans, Green & Co., 1938), 214–15.

6. Cited in ibid., 166.

7. Cited in ibid.

8. Cited in Tuchman, *A Distant Mirror,* 326.

9. Cited in ibid., 327.

10. The previous seven quotations are cited in Jørgensen, *Saint Catherine of Siena,* 232–46.

11. Cited in Tuchman, *A Distant Mirror,* 327.

7. MATTEO RICCI

1. Lewis Hanke, *Aristotle and the American Indians: A Study of Race Prejudice in the Modern World* (London: Hollis & Carter, 1959), 16.

2. Andrew Ross, *A Vision Betrayed: The Jesuits in Japan and China, 1542–1742* (Maryknoll, N.Y.: Orbis Books, 1994), 132.

3. Cited in ibid., 153.

4. Cited in Arnold H. Rowbotham, *Missionary and Mandarin: The Jesuits at the Court of China* (New York: Russell & Russell, 1966), 66.

5. Cited in ibid., 185.

6. Cited in ibid., 176.

7. Cited in Ross, *A Vision Betrayed,* 197.

8. Cited in Rowbotham, *Missionary and Mandarin,* 174–75.

9. Cited in J. Robert Dionne, *The Papacy and the Church* (New York: Philosophical Library, 1987), 87.

10. "Declaration on the Relationship of the Church to Non-Christian Religions," in *The Documents of Vatican II,* ed. Walter M. Abbott (New York: America Press, 1966), no. 2.

11. "Decree on the Missionary Activity of the Church," in Abbott, ed., *The Documents of Vatican II,* nos. 9, 11.

12. Pope John Paul II, *Redemptor hominis,* no. 20.

8. HILDEGARD OF BINGEN

1. Cited in Barbara Newman, *Sister of Wisdom: St. Hildegard's Theology of the Feminine* (Berkeley: University of California Press, 1987), 30.

2. Cited in ibid., 13.

3. Cited in ibid., 6.

4. Cited in ibid., 203.

5. Ibid., 16.

6. Ibid., 41.

7. Proverbs 8:23–25.

8. Wisdom 7:25–26.

9. Cited in Newman, *Sister of Wisdom,* 43.

10. Quotations in this section are cited in ibid., 27–82.

11. Nancy Fierro, *Hildegard of Bingen and Her Vision of the Feminine* (Kansas City: Sheed & Ward, 1994), 27.

12. Newman, *Sister of Wisdom,* 87.

13. Cited in ibid., 49.

14. Fierro, *Hildegard of Bingen,* 19.

15. Ecclesiasticus 9:8; 42:9; 25:24.

16. Cited in Maureen Fiedler and Linda Rabben, eds., *Rome Has Spoken: A Guide to Forgotten Papal Statements and How They Have Changed through the Centuries* (New York: Crossroad, 1998), 119.

17. Cited in Newman, *Sister of Wisdom,* 91.

18. Cited in ibid., 98–99.

19. Cited in ibid., 118.

20. *Catechism of the Catholic Church* (New York: Doubleday, 1995), no. 370.

21. Cited in Elizabeth A. Johnson, *She Who Is: The Mystery of God in Feminist Theological Discourse* (New York: Crossroad, 1992), 172.

22. Cited in Elsa Tamez, ed., *Through Her Eyes: Women's Theology from Latin America* (Maryknoll, N.Y.: Orbis Books, 1989), 62.

23. "Pastoral Constitution on the Church in the Modern World," in *The Documents of Vatican II,* ed. Walter M. Abbott (New York: America Press, 1966), no. 9.

24. "Dogmatic Constitution on Divine Revelation," in Abbott, ed., *The Documents of Vatican II,* no. 8.

25. Cited in Matthew Fox, *Illuminations of Hildegard of Bingen* (Santa Fe, N.Mex.: Bear & Company, 1985), 9.

26. Fierro, *Hildegard of Bingen,* 41.

9. YVES CONGAR

1. Yves Congar, *Dialogue between Christians: Catholic Contributions to Ecumenism* (Westminster, Md.: Newman Press, 1966), 43.

2. Cited in Maureen Fiedler and Linda Rabben, eds., *Rome Has Spoken: A Guide to Forgotten Papal Statements and How They Have Changed through the Centuries* (New York: Crossroad, 1998), 56.

3. Cited in ibid., 57.

4. Cited in ibid.

5. Yves Congar, *Divided Christendom: A Catholic Study of the Problem of Reunion,* trans. M. A. Bousfield (London: Geoffrey Bles, 1966), 40.

6. Ibid., 45.

7. Cited in Aidan Nichols, *Yves Congar* (Wilton, Conn.: Morehouse-Barlow, 1989), 175–78.

8. Pope Pius XII, *Humani generis,* nos. 11–12.

9. Cited in Oscar Arnal, *Priests in Working-Class Blue: The History of the Worker-Priests (1943–1954)* (New York: Paulist Press, 1986), 23.

10. Cited in ibid., 150.

11. Congar, *Dialogue between Christians,* 3.

12. Ibid., 11.

13. Ibid., 21.

14. Ibid., 23.

15. The three preceding quotations are from ibid., 34–38.

16. Ibid., 44.

17. Cited in Yves Congar, *Fifty Years of Catholic Theology: Conversations with Yves Congar,* ed. Bernard Lauret (Philadelphia: Fortress, 1988), 76.

18. "Decree on Ecumenism," in *The Documents of Vatican II,* ed. Walter M. Abbott (New York: America Press, 1966), nos. 3, 4, 6.

19. Yves Congar, *Blessed Is the Peace of My Church,* trans. Salvator Attanasio (Denville, N.J.: Dimension Books, 1973), 102–3.

10. CREATIVE DIFFERENCES

1. Cited in Aloys Grillmeier, *Christ in Christian Tradition: From the Apostolic Age to Chalcedon (451),* trans. John Bowden (London: A. R. Mowbray, 1965), 348.

2. Ibid., 350.

3. Cited in ibid., 352.

4. The full, complex drama is explained in Henry Chadwick, *The Early Church* (London: Penguin Books, 1967), 192–212.

5. Cited in Richard P. McBrien, *Catholicism* (San Francisco: HarperSanFrancisco, 1994), 477.

6. William La Due, *The Chair of Saint Peter: A History of the Papacy* (Maryknoll, N.Y.: Orbis Books, 1999), 83.

7. "Dogmatic Constitution on the Church," in *The Documents of Vatican II,* ed. Walter M. Abbott (New York: America Press, 1966), nos. 22, 26, 27.

8. Pope John Paul II, *Fides et ratio,* no. 43.

9. Josef Pieper, *Guide to Thomas Aquinas,* trans. Richard and Clara Winston (New York: Random House, 1962), 41.

10. Cited in Charles Curran and Robert Hunt, eds., *Dissent in and for the Church: Theologians and Humanae Vitae* (New York: Sheed & Ward, 1969), 71–72.

11. Pieper, *Guide to Thomas Aquinas,* 40.

12. Ibid., 41.

13. Cited in ibid., 41.

14. Thomas O'Meara, *Thomas Aquinas: Theologian* (Notre Dame, Ind.: University of Notre Dame Press, 1997), 13.

15. Pope John Paul II, *Fides et ratio,* no. 44.

16. George Tavard, *Juana Inés de la Cruz and the Theology of Beauty: The First Mexican Theology* (Notre Dame, Ind.: University of Notre Dame Press, 1991), 12.

17. Juana Inés de la Cruz, *A Woman of Genius: The Intellectual Autobiography of Sor Juana Inés de la Cruz,* trans. Margaret Sayers Peden (Salisbury, Conn.: Lime Rock Press, 1982), 28.

18. All quotations in this section are from ibid., 64–88.

19. Cited in Maureen Fiedler and Linda Rabben, eds., *Rome Has Spoken: A Guide to Forgotten Papal Statements and How They Have Changed through the Centuries* (New York: Crossroad, 1998), 84.

20. Cited in Madeleine Hooke Rice, *American Catholic Opinion in the Slavery Controversy* (New York: Columbia University Press, 1944), 67.

21. Cited in ibid., 77.

22. Cited in ibid., 126.

23. Cited in Cyprian Davis, *The History of Black Catholics in the United States* (New York: Crossroad, 1990), 117.

24. Cited in Rice, *American Catholic Opinion,* 121.

25. Cited in Davis, *The History of Black Catholics,* 49.

26. Cited in Rice, *American Catholic Opinion,* 127–28.

27. Cited in ibid., 129.

28. Rice, *American Catholic Opinion,* 130.

29. Cited in Fiedler and Rabben, eds., *Rome Has Spoken,* 84.

30. Cited in ibid., 83.

11. STANDING FIRM

1. Lesley O'Brien, *Mary MacKillop Unveiled* (North Blackburn, Victoria, Australia: CollinsDove, 1994), 132.

2. Cited in Clare Dunne, *Mary MacKillop: No Plaster Saint* (Sydney: ABC Books, 1994), 20–22.

3. Cited in ibid., 23–24.

4. Ibid.

5. Cited in ibid., 48.

6. Cited in O'Brien, *Mary MacKillop Unveiled,* 185.

7. Cited in Brian Tierney, "Limits to Obedience in the 13th Century," in *Contraception: Authority and Dissent,* ed. Charles E. Curran (New York: Herder and Herder, 1969), 76.

8. Cited in ibid., 81.

9. Ibid., 88.

10. Ibid., 100.

11. Cited in ibid., 130.

12. Cited in Penny Blaker Mitchell, *Mother Theodore Guerin: A Woman for Our Time* (St. Mary-of-the-Woods, Ind.: Sisters of Providence, 1987), 90.

13. The remaining quotations in this section are cited in ibid., 92–104.

AFTERWORD

1. Yves Congar, *Blessed Is the Peace of My Church,* trans. Salvator Attanasio (Denville, N.J.: Dimension Books, 1973), 102.

2. Job 10:2–3; 13:5–6; 30:20–21; 42:5.

3. William Safire, *The First Dissident: The Book of Job in Today's Politics* (New York: Random House, 1992), 88.

INDEX

Robert McClory is an associate professor at the Medill School of Journalism, Northwestern University. He has been writing on religion for more than thirty years in the *National Catholic Reporter, U.S. Catholic* magazine, and other publications. He has also written widely on race relations and urban issues in the *Chicago Reader, Chicago* magazine, and *Illinois Issues.* He is the author of two earlier books dealing with Catholic Church history: *Turning Point: The Inside Story of the Papal Birth Control Commission* (Crossroad, 1995) and *Power and the Papacy: The People and Politics behind the Doctrine of Infallibility* (Triumph-Ligouri, 1997).